Online Social Networking

by Carla Mooney

LUCENT BOOKS

A part of Gale, Cengage Learning

GALE
CENGAGE Learning™

Detroit • New York • San Francisco • New Haven, Conn • Waterville, Maine • London

GALE
CENGAGE Learning

LIBRARY OF CONGRESS CATALOGING-IN-PUBLICATION DATA

Mooney, Carla, 1970-
  Online social networking / by Carla Mooney.
     p. cm. -- (Hot topics)
  Includes bibliographical references and index.
  ISBN 978-1-4205-0120-9 (hardcover)
  1. Online social networks--Juvenile literature. 2. Internet and teenagers--Juvenile literature. I. Title.
  HM742.M66 2009
  302.30285--dc22

2008052816

Lucent Books
27500 Drake Rd.
Farmington Hills, MI 48331

ISBN-13: 978-1-4205-0120-9
ISBN-10: 1-4205-0120-8

3 9082 11399 3631

Printed in the United States of America
1 2 3 4 5 6 7 13 12 11 10 09

CONTENTS

FOREWORD

Young people today are bombarded with information. Aside from traditional sources such as newspapers, television, and the radio, they are inundated with a nearly continuous stream of data from electronic media. They send and receive e-mails and instant messages, read and write online "blogs," participate in chat rooms and forums, and surf the Web for hours. This trend is likely to continue. As Patricia Senn Breivik, the former dean of university libraries at Wayne State University in Detroit, has stated, "Information overload will only increase in the future. By 2020, for example, the available body of information is expected to double every 73 days! How will these students find the information they need in this coming tidal wave of information?"

Ironically, this overabundance of information can actually impede efforts to understand complex issues. Whether the topic is abortion, the death penalty, gay rights, or obesity, the deluge of fact and opinion that floods the print and electronic media is overwhelming. The news media report the results of polls and studies that contradict one another. Cable news shows, talk radio programs, and newspaper editorials promote narrow viewpoints and omit facts that challenge their own political biases. The World Wide Web is an electronic minefield where legitimate scholars compete with the postings of ordinary citizens who may or may not be well-informed or capable of reasoned argument. At times, strongly worded testimonials and opinion pieces both in print and electronic media are presented as factual accounts.

Conflicting quotes and statistics can confuse even the most diligent researchers. A good example of this is the question of whether or not the death penalty deters crime. For instance, one study found that murders decreased by nearly one-third when the death penalty was reinstated in New York in 1995. Death penalty supporters cite this finding to support their argument that the existence of the death penalty deters criminals from committing murder. However, another study found that states without the death penalty have murder rates below the national average. This study is cited by opponents of capital punishment, who reject the claim that the death penalty deters murder. Students need context and clear, informed discussion if they are to think critically and make informed decisions.

The Hot Topics series is designed to help young people wade through the glut of fact, opinion, and rhetoric so that they can think critically about controversial issues. Only by reading and thinking critically will they be able to formulate a viewpoint that is not simply the parroted views of others. Each volume of the series focuses on one of today's most pressing social issues and provides a balanced overview of the topic. Carefully crafted narrative, fully documented primary and secondary source quotes, informative sidebars, and study questions all provide excellent starting points for research and discussion. Full-color photographs and charts enhance all volumes in the series. With its many useful features, the Hot Topics series is a valuable resource for young people struggling to understand the pressing issues of the modern era.

INTRODUCTION

THE EXPLOSION OF ONLINE SOCIAL NETWORKING

In recent years the use of online social networking has sky-rocketed. Social networks were once a niche activity for teenagers. Now social networking absorbs tens of millions of Internet users. People of all ages, races, and ethnic backgrounds interact on social networks. Ordinary people log on to profiles, chat online with friends, and upload their latest vacation pictures.

Cost is no longer a barrier to social network use. Computers and Internet access are more affordable than ever. Libraries offer free portals to the online world. Geographic barriers have also fallen. It is easy and inexpensive to chat online with friends from Asia to Australia. Suddenly, anyone can become someone online.

One factor in the explosive growth of sites like MySpace and Facebook is the shift in attitudes about social networking. Users no longer see these sites as just online bulletin boards. They treat the sites as if they are actual places, somewhere to meet and hang out. While past generations met friends and socialized at the mall or movie theater, more of this behavior is moving online.

In addition the introduction of multimedia capabilities to social networks has enthralled users. For the first time in history, the average Internet user can upload pictures, music, and video to Web pages with ease. With these new tools, users can creatively express themselves online as never before. Displays of art, music, and writing abound on social network sites, each one unique to its creator.

The adult world has also embraced social networking. Businesses, politicians, schools, libraries, and activists have discovered the power of social networks to change the way they work. While teens may view social networks as "their space," it has quickly become "our space" for the world.

Many people believe that the growing use of social networks will have an impact on society. Worldwide networks will introduce new ideas and cultures to a widening audience. Collaboration and cooperation across groups and countries will be easier than ever. Some people argue, however, that too much time in front of a computer keyboard will have a negative impact. They question whether young people will develop adequate face-to-face communication skills. Others point out that as people feel

The popularity of sites such as MySpace and Facebook has made online social networking a cultural phenomenon, changing the way people connect and communicate with each other.

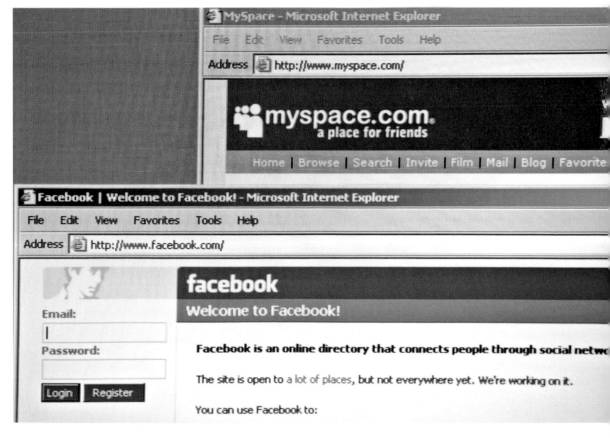

less inhibited behind a computer screen, they may be more likely to participate in cyberbullying. Some young people, especially girls, may post increasingly sexual pictures of themselves and add graphic sexual comments to their profiles. Some people worry that this online sexualization may lead to promiscuous behavior offline and attract dangerous attention from predators.

In recent years the media spotlight on social networking has brought some complex issues to the forefront. All communities, whether online or offline, have a darker side and must deal with safety. Social networks are no exception. Dangers such as predators, drugs, and pornography lurk online. Countless cases of young people being lured by these elements abound in the news. Predators groom teens in chat rooms and convince them to meet offline. Students link up with drug dealers through social network friends to buy drugs. Tweens stumble onto pornographic pictures by following a link on a new friend's social network profile.

The ease with which users can run into trouble online concerns many adults. Some parents, schools, and legislators have called for the banning of these sites. "I talk to parents all the time about the need to educate themselves," said Ron Wenkart, general counsel for the Orange County Department of Education. "If they knew what their kids were up to, many of them would be horrified."[1] Other groups protest that banning is rarely effective. Instead, they believe adults have a responsibility to educate young people about social networking safety.

Another concern is the erosion of personal privacy as more information lands online. As people post their inner thoughts for the world to see, some people are very concerned by this abandonment of privacy. With teachers, colleges, and employers looking online, users may risk their reputations and futures over a few pictures of partying with friends. High school teacher Tom Goldsbury believes that students do not fully understand the long-term consequences of revealing personal details online. He says, "There's this youthful bravado, 'Nothing bad can happen to me.'"[2]

In other cases privacy may be violated without the user even knowing it. Once a picture or post goes online, users are powerless to stop others from cutting and pasting their content to other sites. In addition some applications to enhance social network profiles require users to share personal information with the application developer. Once that information is in the developer's hands, the user has once again lost control and privacy.

The supporters of online social networks believe that despite the risks, social networking can be good for society. "We need to keep in mind that the benefits of this interactive technology far outweigh the risks," said Robert Leri, a school district technology and information director. "When it's used in a positive way, it can be an extraordinary tool."[3]

WHAT IS ONLINE SOCIAL NETWORKING?

People connect online in many ways. Social networking sites, e-mail, instant messaging, video- and photo-sharing sites, and comment posting are all tools that help people communicate and socialize with each other. Each connection is a piece of the larger arena of online social networking. Broadly defined, online social networking is a Web site or other type of online communication that allows people to interact with each other. People's experiences with social networking, however, are as different as the choices they make online.

Building the Foundation

Online social networking would not be possible without the Internet and the World Wide Web. The Internet evolved through the efforts of several government agencies and university scientists. To ease communications between computers at universities and research centers, they devised a way for computers on the different networks to "talk." This system of communication eventually became the Internet. As the Internet grew, it connected millions of computers around the globe and formed a communication network. The development of the Internet laid the infrastructure for social networking.

Early Internet applications allowed people to communicate in small groups through closed networks. As the Internet grew and became an open network, the number of people using the network increased. They could connect more freely and publicly than ever before.

Early Internet use was not as simple as it would become in later years. Telephone lines and modems connected computers physically to the Internet. However, actually getting the information out of the Internet was not simple. Web sites or Web pages did not exist. Data sharing was not user-friendly. Without a technical background, information was difficult to find.

Introducing the World Wide Web

Using the Internet became easier in 1991 with the launch of the World Wide Web. The Web was a new system designed to create, organize, and link documents and Web pages so that people could easily read them over the Internet. While the Internet was the system of networks to connect people, the World Wide Web provided the means for people to use that connectivity.

British computer scientist Tim Berners-Lee designed the World Wide Web. He created the HTML coding system for Web pages and the addressing system that gave each Web page a specific location, or URL. The World Wide Web brought the Internet alive.

The invention of HTML (hypertext markup language) coding allowed the display of content on the World Wide Web.

The next step in creating an easy-to-use Internet was the development of the Web browser. Browser software communicated with the Internet. The software translated Web pages and data into an easy-to-read format on computer screens. Browsers such as Netscape and Internet Explorer helped people of all ages and backgrounds use the Internet. The creation of the World Wide Web and Web browsers enabled the Internet to grow at a rapid pace. By 2006, 73 percent of American adults were Internet users.

For most of the 1990s, the Web was a provider of information. Companies and organizations registered Web addresses and created Web sites to provide information to the public. People used this information passively. They read and absorbed it, but did little to add to or change what they found online.

Web Use Begins to Change

Around 2002 the way in which people used the Internet and World Wide Web began to change. A trend emerged of users creating and uploading their own content onto the Web. The term "Web 2.0" surfaced to describe this second level of use for the World Wide Web.

Although the underlying technology of the Web had not changed, the change in how people used it made the Web more interactive. People could post writing, pictures, video, and music on the Web and invite others to view and comment on them. They were no longer just absorbing the information in front of them. Now they were creating and adding to it. This dramatic change in the Internet's use opened up a whole new world of possibilities. People were eager to join in and explore.

In the interactive Web 2.0 environment, online social networking took hold. Social networking was fluid. Its form was constantly changing and being updated. Through it all, the primary goal of online networking users was to socialize with other people. The form people chose to use was simply a tool to help them achieve their goal.

Blogging Online

Some of the earliest social networking occurred on blogs. A blog is a Web page that functions as an online journal or diary. Blog

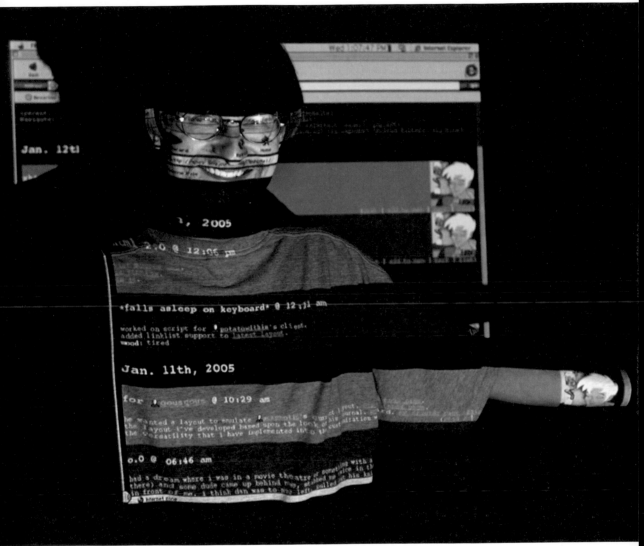

A blogger stands in front of a projected image of his entries on LiveJournal, one of the first blogging Web sites.

sites created tools that let users easily post entries and photos on a personal Web page. The blogger did not need specific technical knowledge to post content on the Web page. Instead, most blog tools made posting as simple as using a basic word processing program. Suddenly, almost anyone could post content to his or her own Web page.

Interview with Author and Blogger Mio Debham

On choosing a blog: "As a writer, it was a toss up between maintaining a website or a blog. Ultimately I decided to go with the blog. It's a way to raise your profile and also to maintain a habit of writing regularly . . . people who aren't aware of me as a writer can see that I am able to write, and hopefully can see that I have a sense of humour!"

On posting: "I post once a week . . . when people visit your website or blog you get one chance of a return visit . . . if they visit the next time and it has been static you've pretty much blown the chance of another return trip."

On the positives: "A few 'strangers' have written to me to say they enjoyed reading my blog . . . which is nice. It allows the friends I don't write to often enough to have a hint of what I'm up to. . . . Also I've raised my profile—I've had a few job offers recently where they have said they've read and enjoyed the blog."

E-mail to author, June 26, 2008.

Early bloggers posted diary entries for other users to read. As social networking evolved, the blog sites added features to make the experience more interactive. Readers now had the ability to respond to blog entries by posting comments to the blogger. The blogger, in turn, could reply to the post in another comment or diary entry.

LiveJournal was one of the first blogging Web sites. Founder Brad Fitzpatrick founded the site in 1999. He originally designed it as a tool to keep in touch with friends. Prior to blogging Web sites like LiveJournal, bloggers needed a lot of technical skill and patience to post blogs. The introduction of LiveJournal made blogging much simpler for the average user. LiveJournal also carried a strong social element to its blog by allowing users to keep a "friends" list. Via a Friends page, users could check in on their friends' latest journal posts. LiveJournal did not have the multimedia features of other social networking sites, which made it a less popular choice for teens.

Social Networking Sites

At the same time that blogging's appeal was growing, some pure social networking sites appeared. These sites encouraged online social connections. Early sites such as SixDegrees.com and Friendster allowed people to manage a list of friends. One drawback to these sites was that they did not offer users the ability to publish content like blogs.

Friendster founder Jonathan Abrams poses with a T-shirt promoting the online social networking site, one of the first of its kind.

Social networking sites begin with a group of founders sending out messages to friends to join the network. In turn the friends send out messages to their friends, and the network grows. When members join the network, they create a profile. Depending on the site, users can customize their profile to reflect their interests. They also begin to have contact with friends, acquaintances, and strangers.

BREAKING DOWN TECHNICAL BARRIERS

"When you give people a new way to connect with other people, they will punch through any technical barrier, they will learn new languages—people are wired to want to connect with other people." —Marc Andreessen, software engineer and cofounder of Netscape Communications Corporation.

Quoted in Thomas L. Friedman, *The World Is Flat: A Brief History of the Twenty-first Century.* New York: Farrar, Straus & Giroux, 2006, p. 68.

Founded in 2002, Friendster used the model of friends inviting friends to join in order to grow its network. It quickly signed on millions of users. Unfortunately, as the site grew larger, technical issues surfaced. Painfully slow servers made it difficult for users to move around the site. Additionally, management enforced strict policies on fake profiles. These false profiles, or "fakesters," as they were known, were deleted by the site. This approach turned off users. Eventually, Friendster began to lose members in the United States.

Fellow networking site SixDegrees.com closed its doors after the dot-com bust in 2000. Within a few years, these early social networking sites found their popularity declining. At the same time, a new social networking site called MySpace was beginning to take off.

The Rise of MySpace

MySpace brought together the social features of networking sites and the publishing capabilities of blogs. The combination of the

MySpace founders Tom Anderson and Chris DeWolfe originally launched the site, currently the most trafficked on the Internet, in 2003 as a place for artists and fans to promote music.

two tools struck a home run with teens. Young people were look-ing for a more social way to blog. MySpace provided the solution.

In 2003 Tom Anderson and Chris DeWolfe launched My-Space in Santa Monica, California. As music fans, the pair de-signed the site as a place to promote local music acts. They also wanted to be able to connect with other fans and friends.

On MySpace, users created a Web page with a personal pro-file. Then they invited other users to become their friends. Ac-cording to DeWolfe, the bands were a great marketing tool in the beginning. He said: "All these creative people became ambas-sadors for MySpace by using us as their de facto promotional platform. People like to talk about music, so the bands set up a natural environment to communicate."[4]

THE POPULARITY OF SOCIAL NETWORKS

"With social networks, there's a fascination with intimacy because it simulates face-to-face communication. But there's also this fun-damental distance. That distance makes it safe for people to con-nect through weak ties where they can have the appearance of a connection because it's safe." —Michael Wesch, teacher of cultural anthropology at Kansas State University.

Quoted in Alex Wright, "Friending, Ancient or Otherwise," *New York Times*, December 2, 2007.

Anderson and DeWolfe were determined to keep MySpace an open site. Anyone could join the community, browse profiles, and post whatever they wanted. User control was one of their founding principles. It also made initial financing hard to find. According to Anderson: "We'd get calls from investor types who wanted to meet us. They would say 'Your site isn't professional. Why do you let users control the pages? They're so ugly!'"[5]

In the meantime MySpace continued to sign people up. Teens and young adults loved the site. They flocked to create their own profiles. The ability to customize pages, load music, and share videos added to the MySpace appeal.

Unlike other early social networking sites, MySpace gave users a media-rich experience. Users could express themselves on their Web page by adding music and video clips. At the same time, they could socialize with friends. MySpace made social contact easier with tools such as e-mail, comment posts, chat rooms, buddy lists, discussion boards, and instant messaging. MySpace brought together the ability to express oneself and to socialize in one place.

The timing was perfect. Over the next two years, MySpace grew at a tremendous pace. The site's success brought attention from investors. Rupert Murdoch, famous for his media empire, wanted to buy MySpace. Murdoch had interests in television, film, newspapers, publishing, and the Internet. In 2005 Murdoch purchased MySpace for an amazing $580 million.

By early 2008 MySpace had grown to a mind-blowing 110 million active users. It signed an average of thirty thousand people up every day. One in four Americans was on MySpace. The Web site had become the giant among social networking sites. It was the most trafficked site on the Internet.

MySpace's influence traveled outside of the United States. The company built a local presence in over twenty international territories. MySpace could be found in places such as the United Kingdom, Japan, Australia, and Latin America. In a few short years, MySpace had become a worldwide cultural phenomenon.

Social Networking Beyond MySpace

The success of MySpace in the social networking arena spurred the development and redesign of many other online social networks. Some sites appealed to a general audience. Others, such as Black Planet, LinkedIn, and MyChurch, sought to serve a niche market.

Facebook was one site that emerged as an alternative to MySpace. In February 2004 Harvard student Mark Zuckerberg launched Facebook. The site began as a closed network for college students. Closed networks only allow users to join if they meet certain criteria. In contrast, sites such as MySpace and Friendster were open social networking sites. Anyone could sign up for an account.

While an undergraduate at Harvard University, Facebook founder Mark Zuckerberg launched the site in 2004 as a closed network for college students.

Open and closed social networks have advantages and disadvantages. Open networks foster interaction between adults and teens. Parents can check up on their teen's profile and decide if they are comfortable with their child's online image. On the other hand, open access means that profiles are completely public and can attract unwanted attention.

Closed networks are generally smaller. As such, there is a greater chance a user will know other members both online and offline. But a closed network blocks parents from reading their teen or college student's profile. Being closed also limits a social network's ability to grow and attract new users.

As a closed college network, Facebook grew by adding more colleges to its network. By the end of 2004, Facebook had almost

1 million active users. As Facebook's popularity grew, it expanded beyond colleges to high school and international school users. At this point, however, the site was still restricted to a limited pool of student users.

In 2006 Facebook made a pivotal decision. It opened the network to the general public, expanding beyond its original student base. By May 2008 Facebook boasted over 70 million active users. At that time, it was the second-most trafficked social networking site behind MySpace and the sixth-most trafficked site on the Web.

As an alternative to MySpace, Facebook's social network gained popularity with business professionals and colleagues. Facebook's purpose was to help users connect online with people that they already knew offline. Unlike the wild-looking pages found on MySpace, Facebook promoted a clean, orderly online experience.

Video- and Photo-Sharing Sites

Online social networking evolved into a full multimedia experience with the arrival of video- and photo-sharing Web sites. Users could upload visual content to share with friends and other users.

Photo-sharing sites such as Flickr enabled users to transfer digital photos online to share with others. Users decided whether to share their photos publicly or limit access to private groups. Users could also use the site's features to organize and store pictures and video.

One of the most popular video-sharing Web sites was YouTube. The site, founded in 2005, used Adobe Flash technology to display clips from movies and television, music videos, and video blogs. Users could upload, share, and view video clip topics from the latest movies to funny moments captured on film.

Not everyone wanted to create a profile, write a blog, or upload pictures and video. Other social networking tools allowed these users to participate online. E-mails sent messages to a friend's electronic mailbox. Instant messaging was a real-time conversation between two people online at the same time. Comment posting allowed users to interact and talk about a friend's blog, profile, or pictures. Even online gaming was a form of social networking, allowing players to meet other people with similar interests online.

Why Is Online Social Networking So Popular?

The popularity of online social networking has prompted researchers to explore the similarities between online social networks and tribal societies. According to Lance Strate, a communications professor at Fordham University, social networks appeal to people because they feel more like talking than writing. "Orality is the base of all human experience," said Strate. "We evolved with speech. We didn't evolve with writing."[6]

Irwin Chen, an instructor at Parsons design school, is developing a new course to explore oral culture online. He agrees with Strate. "Orality is participatory, interactive, communal and focused on the present," he says. "The Web is all of these things."[7]

Evaluating Web Sites

Web 2.0 has ushered in an era where ordinary people upload content to Web sites, blogs, and profiles. Is anyone looking to make sure the content they provide is correct? Web 2.0 enables a nursery school teacher to write an accounting blog. A karate teacher could film a cooking video clip. Increasingly, the responsibility of evaluating the accuracy of Web information falls on the user's shoulders. The following are useful items to look for when evaluating Web information.

- Who is the author and what are his or her credentials?
- Is the information from a known and respected source?
- Can you contact the author?
- Can you confirm the information with another source? Is the information documented with cited sources?
- Is the information current?
- If there are links on the site, do they work? Do they link to reputable sources?
- What level of accuracy is needed?
- Is the site fair and objective? Or is it biased toward one side of an issue?
- Is the site designed for information or for recreational purposes?
- Does the Web site creator benefit in some way from the information presented?

Frances Jacobson Harris, "Elements of Web Site Evaluation," University Laboratory High School Library, November 2007. www.uni.uiuc.edu/library/computer lit/evaluation.php.

Michael Wesch teaches cultural anthropology at Kansas State University. He studied how people form social relationships while living with a tribe in Papua New Guinea. He compared the tribe to online social networking. "In tribal cultures, your identity is completely wrapped up in the question of how people know you," he said. "When you look at Facebook, you can see the same pattern at work: people projecting their identities by demonstrating their relationships to each other. You define yourself in terms of who your friends are."[8]

Despite the connections between social networks and tribal cultures, significant differences exist. In tribal societies relationships form through face-to-face contact. Social networks allow users to hide behind a computer screen. Tribal societies embrace formal rituals. Social networks value a casual approach to relationships.

Millions of people across the world have joined online social networks. Perhaps their popularity stems from our innate desire to be part of a community. According to Strate, social networking "fulfills our need to be recognized as human beings, and as members of a community. We all want to be told: You exist."[9]

CHAPTER 2

TEENS AND ONLINE SOCIAL NETWORKING

Millions of teens participate in social networks. According to the 1997 Pew Research report *Teens and Social Media*, 93 percent of teens are active online. Fifty-five percent have created a profile on a social networking site. What are teens doing on these sites? Why are they spending so much time connecting with others online?

Hanging Out Moves Online

Ask teens what they do on social networking sites and chances are their answer will be "just hang out." In fact, hanging out with friends is nothing new to generations of teenagers. Parents of today's teens remember gathering with friends at the local mall or diner. This behavior is a normal part of adolescents becoming adults. Socializing with friends teaches teens how to interact with others. They learn society's norms and rules. According to researcher Danah Boyd, hanging out is "how youth get socialized into peer groups. Hanging out amongst friends allows teens to build relationships and stay connected."[10]

How Teens Are Using Online Networks

"What you see is all the behaviors you should recognize from your own teenage years. The difference is that now it's less physical and more word based." —Danah Boyd, Berkeley doctoral candidate and researcher of children's online social practices.

Quoted in Michelle Andrews, "Decoding MySpace," *U.S. News & World Report*, September 10, 2006. www.usnews.com/usnews/news/articles/060910///18myspace_print.htm.

Teens hang out at a diner in the 1950s, when social connections among young people were largely based on face-to-face contact.

Past generations enjoyed hours after school to gather with friends. Today's teens find themselves with less time and fewer opportunities to hang out. Teens fill their schedules with sports practices, theater rehearsals, extra study sessions, or other activities. The physical space where they can hang out has also changed. Many public places such as the mall and local parks have added strict rules to limit unsupervised teens on-site. With less time and opportunity available for hanging out, teens have turned to the Web.

The Web has become a virtual hangout. It is a place to connect with friends after school. On the Web, teens can interact away from parents. David Huffaker, a researcher of online social behavior at Northwestern University, wrote in an academic paper that "these activities are important for identity exploration, which is one of the principal tasks of adolescence."[11]

Fulfilling Adolescent Needs

Teenagers struggle daily to maneuver the road to adulthood. Along the way, they face several developmental needs to prepare them for life beyond the teen years. While hanging out is not new, the technology of online social networking has created new and exciting ways for teens to meet their needs.

Connecting and Communicating with Friends

Long gone are the days of waiting to use the telephone. Teens chat using instant messaging for hours. They log on to each other's profiles to post comments and keep current on the latest happenings. They post bulletins about what is new. They share details of their lives, talk about concerns, and even get help with school. Online social networks such as MySpace give teens a variety of ways to connect with friends. These networks also enable them to reach many more people in less time.

Just like in high school, cliques and groups form online. Most teens choose to communicate with peers within their own social circle. This practice existed well before the introduction of online social networking. It is similar to the unwritten seating chart in the school cafeteria, where the athletes sit in one section and the drama kids gather in another. Online networks are the larger social scene in which teens find their own groups. Teens' experiences with social networks are in large part determined by the company they keep online, who their friends are, and who they allow into their group.

The term *friends* takes on a new meaning in online social networks. On sites such as MySpace, teens receive invitations from other users to become friends. Once accepted, friends have access to virtually all content on the teen's profile. Teens also rank their friends, frequently displaying the top four or eight names on their profile. This type of ranking can lead to social competition and hurt feelings, as higher rankings are often linked to higher social standing.

A Place to Express Oneself

The teenage years are a time of discovery. Teens learn about self, interests, and talents. Self-expression gives teens an outlet to find who they are and where they want to go in life. Author Brenda Ueland wrote in 1938: "Everybody is talented because everybody who is human has something to express. Try not expressing anything for twenty-four hours and see what happens. You will nearly burst."[12]

Online social networking gives teens new tools to express themselves. Teen writers create poetry and verse on blogs. Artists post pictures of their work on Web pages. Photographers display digital images. Actors and musicians upload videos of skits and performances for others to view.

An important piece of self-expression is feedback from others. Teens want to know that others are paying attention to them. Online social networks provide instant feedback to teens. Users can rate or comment on poetry, artwork, or music. Positive feedback encourages teens to develop their unique talents and abilities. Online, teens can find the support and encouragement that they may be missing in a hectic world.

A Pew Internet & American Life Project study released in December 2007 found that 64 percent of online teens participated in content creation on the Internet. In addition social networking sites are the centers for teen content. A teen's profile on MySpace is the perfect place to share his or her creations with friends and others. Sharing pictures and video content is widely

Because online social networks enable the creation of original content, teens use them as a forum for self-expression, sharing their music, creative writing, and art with the online world.

popular with teens. Most teens report they frequently receive comments on their photo and video content, often sparking an online conversation.

Susannah Stern, an assistant professor at the University of San Diego, researches adolescents' Internet use. She has found that teens have created a rich online world. "It's just marvelous—just very creative, artistic, opinioned, thoughtful," she says. "They're clearly putting a lot of time into their Internet expression, whether it's in the form of a blog or a homepage or instant message or away message."[13]

The Pew study also found that blogging has become more popular with teens, especially older teen girls. Mike Riera, author and expert on adolescent development, believes that online tools such as blogging help teens discover who they are. He says, "They're [also] discovering insights and formulating opinion on things and experiencing the evolution of their thinking, and so [blogging] allows them to document this."[14]

Getting Together

Teenagers thrive on going out and doing things with friends. Social networks such as MySpace have taken planning online. Teens can announce events such as parties, school functions, and even small get-togethers online. MySpace tools help teens send invitations to their friend list, receive RSVPs, and keep an online guest list. Even details such as directions can be posted or linked online.

Beyond private parties, teens use social networks to search for events in their towns that are of interest to them. MySpace displays public events on the Events page under different categories. Teens can browse the postings and decide which ones they want to put on their calendar.

Finding an Identity

Teens are discovering who they are and what their identity in the world will be. Online social networking provides an environment for teens to experiment with their identity. They create profiles based on how they see themselves at the moment.

As that view changes, teens can easily change their online profiles. This ease allows teens to test different identities and create new profiles. According to author Anastasia Goodstein in her book *Totally Wired: What Teens and Tweens Are Really Doing Online*, "Trying on different identities is also simply a part of growing up."[15]

Growing Independence

As teens search for identity, they test their growing independence. They search beyond the inner circle of family and friends to explore and develop personal tastes. Online, teens can explore forums and communities. They can visit chat rooms and listen to discussions. Learning different points of view helps teens develop their own beliefs.

Online, teens can find others who share specific interests like robotics or the environment. Group members share knowledge with each other. Physical location is no longer a barrier. The group may have members from across the country or around the world. Social networks give teens the chance to mingle with peers from different backgrounds and cultures while they develop interests.

EDUCATIONAL BENEFITS OF ONLINE NETWORKING

"Students are developing a positive attitude towards using technology systems, editing and customizing content and thinking about online design and layout. They're also sharing creative original work like poetry and film. . . . The Web sites offer tremendous educational potential." —Christine Greenhow, a learning technologies researcher at the University of Minnesota.

Quoted in University of Minnesota, "First-of-Its-Kind Study at the University of Minnesota Uncovers the Educational Benefits of Social Networking Sites," June 19, 2008. www1.umn.edu/umnnews/news_details.php?release=080619_3591&page=UMNN.

Although forums and chat rooms provide an opportunity to meet a wider group of people, there are risks involved. In public forums, there are no restrictions on who can enter and post. People are free to say whatever they want in whatever language they choose. Profanity is common in these spaces. Unfortunately, adults with less-than-honorable intentions can sometimes be found lurking in these spaces. Despite these drawbacks, forums and chat rooms can offer teens an intriguing glimpse into a wider world.

Concern About Teens' Negative Behavior

Millions of teens use social networking in a positive way. Unfortunately, with the rise of social networks, negative behaviors associated with the online world have also increased. Some teens have become obsessed with online life, others display sexual pictures and graphic comments, and still others use online tools to bully peers.

Online Obsession

For many teens, checking online messages and bulletin boards can become more than a daily habit. Many teens admit to becoming obsessed with social networking.

A fifteen-year-old girl described MySpace as "a high like no other. I can't wait to sit at my computer and take the day's drama in. I just don't feel compete until I've caught up on the MySpace juice!"[16] Adriana, a graduate student in psychology, agreed. She said, "It can really get addicting. You start to want to stalk people. You kind of follow their every move."[17]

Standing Alone—Offline

Fifteen-year-old Izzy talked about her decision to stay away from social networks:

I did open a Xanga account very early on but closed it pretty quick as I found it dull—not so many people were on it. And by the time it all got popular, there had been a couple of not nice things going on so I thought nah, I'll leave it. Also it's sort of become my niche—I'm the retro person without a facebook account . . . you want to talk to me, you have to call! I also think it's a waste of time . . . people spend hours and hours on it!

They (my friends) used to nag me a lot more about MSN but they don't pressure me much over facebook . . . though they do indirectly when they load things on and tell me I "must" go and see it. But they're pretty good and if it is really something they want me to see (like photos) they will log on and show me on their page. But my drama teacher is really pressuring me to get it because she wants to start up a forum for a project we're doing! She couldn't believe I didn't have facebook.

E-mail to author, June 26, 2008.

Teens may begin to panic when they cannot access their sites. Another fifteen-year-old girl talked about her friend's reaction to losing a MySpace profile: "I once was with a friend whose My-Space was deleted by hackers, and by the way she was acting, one could think that her family dog had died. She was utterly

Some teens describe becoming so hooked on online social networking that they check their sites many times a day and spend much of their free time at their computers.

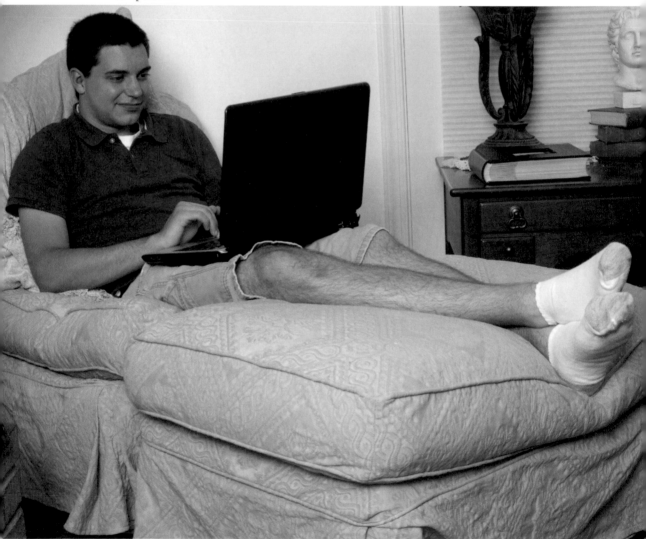

distraught and was going on and on about how long it was going to take her to get it back up like that again."[18]

The symptoms of online obsession can be both psychological and physical. Psychological signs include social withdrawal and problems relating to others. Teens might want to spend more time at the computer, feeling empty or depressed when away from the keyboard. Physical symptoms include dry eyes, carpal tunnel syndrome, migraines, backaches, and sleep disturbances.

While introverted teens are typically at risk for Internet obsessions, extroverted teens may be more at risk for a social networking compulsion. The social component of the sites calls these teens back to the sites again and again.

The cofounder of MySpace, Chris DeWolfe, is not worried about addiction to his site. "I don't think it's a concern at all," he said. "I think it's more substitutional. People are spending less time watching television, and they're spending more time on MySpace."[19]

Online Sexuality

In every era teenagers have sought the attention of the opposite sex. It is a normal and healthy part of adolescent development. Girls worry about how they look. They compare their physical features with other girls, all in a competition for boys' attention. As the girls search for identity, they also seek validation from others. The technology of social networks has created the newest place for girls to achieve this goal.

Online, teens flirt through instant messaging and profile pages. They post pictures and receive instant feedback with online ratings. The sexy photos, taglines, and screen names attract more attention from boys online. The desire for attention and positive feedback leads some girls to post increasingly sexual content. Pictures of girls posing in bikinis, lingerie, and even topless are not uncommon. One fifteen-year-old described her profile: "It only makes sense why so many guys would like to have my picture on their page; I look hot. I'm trying to look as hot as possible, and get as many adds [as a friend to other profiles] as possible."[20]

The increased sexuality may be linked to the effect of today's culture on teens. Sexual images flood music videos, commercials, television, and movies. Teens see the questionable example of celebrities such as Paris Hilton and Britney Spears. An attitude of exhibitionism has become more accepted. Ariel Levy is the author of *Female Chauvinist Pigs: Women and the Rise of Raunch Culture*. She believes that "a baseline expectation that women will be constantly exploding in little blasts of exhibitionism runs throughout our culture. *Girls Gone Wild* is not extraordinary; it's emblematic."[21] Girls have learned to be exhibitionists to get attention, and they push the envelope in fear of being ignored.

GIRLS ON MYSPACE

"Girls on MySpace generate ostentatious displays of sexuality. Clearly they are not empowered, but they really think they are. . . . Unfortunately, the result is a generation of depressed, disconnected, self-mutilating, anorexic young women. It's not a healthy place for girls." —Melanie C. Klein, professor of sociology at California State University, Northridge.

Quoted in Candice M. Kelsey, *Generation MySpace: Helping Your Teen Survive Online Adolescence*. New York: Marlowe, 2007, p. 159.

It remains to be seen if teenage girls are taking their online sexual identities and acting them out in the real world. While experimentation and identity seeking are normal teen behaviors, the amount that some teens expose can be frightening.

Cyberbullying

Social networking has also given traditional bullies a way to move harassment online. Cyberbullying is defined as " bullying that involves the use of e-mail, instant messaging, text messages and digital images sent via cellular phones, Web pages, Web logs (blogs), chat rooms or discussion groups and other information technologies."[22]

The majority of kids have been affected at some point by cyberbullying. i-SAFE America, an organization that promotes Web safety education, studied a group of fourth to eighth graders.

Cyberbullying—Megan's Story

Thirteen-year-old Megan Meier logged on to MySpace to chat with Josh, the new boy she had met online. For a month, the two exchanged e-mails. While Megan's mother was nervous about the online friendship, Megan reassured her that it was okay.

Everything changed when Josh started sending nasty messages to Megan, saying he did not want to be her friend, and posting unflattering things about her on the site's electronic bulletins. Megan, struggling with depression, did not understand why Josh's attitude had suddenly changed. According to her mother, the messages devastated Megan. By the next day, Megan hanged herself in her bedroom closet.

Six weeks after Megan's death, her family learned disturbing news. "Josh" never existed. The mother of one of Megan's former friends had posed as the teenage boy in order to see what Megan was saying about her daughter. The neighbor, Lori Drew, has since been indicted in federal court for her involvement in Megan's death.

In a statement, U.S. Attorney Thomas P. O'Brien said, "Any adult who uses the Internet or a social gathering Web site to bully or harass another person, particularly a young teenage girl, needs to realize that their actions can have serious consequences."

Quoted in CNN.com, "Mom Indicted in Deadly MySpace Hoax," May 15, 2008. www.cnn.com/2008/CRIME/05/15/internet.suicide/index.html.

Tina Meier holds photos of her daughter, Megan, who committed suicide in 2006 after someone she thought was a friend made her the target of nasty e-mail messages and insulting online postings.

They found that 58 percent of these students had mean or hurtful things said to them online. Forty-two percent admitted to being bullied online. The majority of these teens did not tell parents or other adults about the online bullying.

The bullying happened through threatening e-mails, nasty instant messages, and repeated text messages. In some cases, the bully set up Web sites or profiles to make fun of others, impersonated someone else online to post messages, and forwarded private messages, photos, and videos to others.

The biggest difference between traditional and cyberbullying is the anonymous nature of the Internet. Because teens cannot see or hear how their comments affect the person they bully, they are more likely to send increasingly nasty messages. Teen tendencies of weak impulse control and extreme emotional swings also contribute to the rise of cyberbullying.

Online, anyone can bully. Bullies do not have to be physically strong or dominant. Without this barrier, the rate of cyberbullying is much higher than traditional bullying. One school counselor noted that cyberbullying was "the coward's way of bullying because you don't have to have that one-on-one contact . . . you can do it without having that physical reaction."[23]

THE IMPACT OF CYBERBULLYING

"I don't think many adults understand the extent of harm that can be done. We're not talking about some simple e-mails being sent. There's more to this than just a few lines of type and nasty gossip."
—Mother of a bullied child.

Quoted in Candice M. Kelsey, *Generation MySpace: Helping Your Teen Survive Online Adolescence.* New York: Marlowe, 2007, p. 123.

To a victim online bullying can seem endless. Once someone posts an ugly comment or blog about another teen, the harassment does not end there. The posts sit on social networks indefinitely. They can be passed around through links and e-mails. As each new person reads the negative comment or photo, the harassment begins again. This cycle can repeat over weeks, even months.

The effects of cyberbullying on teens can be devastating. Schoolwork may suffer, and sleeping difficulties may surface. Some teens withdraw into depression. Others turn to suicide to end their torment. After two years of being cyberbullied, fifteen-year-old Jeff Johnston hanged himself in his closet. His mother, Debbie, and her husband are now lobbying schools, parents, and politicians to put laws and policies in place to protect other kids.

Cyberbullies use their computers to hurt, humiliate, and threaten others through e-mail, instant messages, and online postings.

Debbie Johnston said: "I'm not the first parent to experience this, but my son had a purpose to his life. And I would like everyone to know that."[24]

Avoiding cyberbullies is not as easy as simply turning off the computer. Teens can block the bully's e-mails, create a new profile or account, and report the bully's offensive behavior to their Internet service provider. Unfortunately, these steps can be time-consuming and may only be a temporary fix. The bully is still online, posting his or her messages in new places where others can see. In addition some people believe that schools should address the issue. Updated policies should include the school's stand on cyberbullying. Schools can hold educational seminars for all students to decrease cyberbullying on campus.

The catch, however, is that the majority of cyberbullying occurs off school property and after school hours. Experts disagree on the role of the school in these instances. How far does their control reach into their students' personal lives before it begins to infringe upon their right to free speech?

As teens embrace social networking, the debate continues over the positive and negative aspects of these sites. The concern over new technology is not new to society. Prior generations believed that reading could hurt young girls and comic books would lead to crime. Understanding the technology and what teens are doing online will help adults recognize and reward the creative ways teens use social networks. As noted by authors Larry Magid and Anne Collier: "We need to understand that the Web, as our teenagers use it, is not just a productivity tool or a more convenient way to find information. . . . It's not a tool as we adults see it. It's an extension of teenagers themselves."[25]

WHO IS RESPONSIBLE FOR SOCIAL NETWORK SAFETY?

Social networking sites are not used by people for benign purposes only. Drug dealers, pornographers, and pedophiles have extended their reach through online social networks, touching more teens than ever before. Extensive media coverage of teens being lured by strangers has stirred concern with adults in the community. Some seek to ban the sites entirely, all in the name of protecting minors. Other experts advocate teaching teens to use social networks responsibly. Whose responsibility is online safety? And do the safety measures cause more harm than good?

Do Not Talk to Strangers

Parents warn their children not to talk to strangers. They give directions on what to do if a stranger approaches them. Run, scream, get away—all are strategies kids and teens learn at home and school. But what if that stranger is not standing on the corner or hanging out next to the playground? What if that stranger uses a MySpace account to find his or her next victim?

In 2004 *Dateline NBC* teamed up with an online justice group called Perverted Justice. Volunteers posed as young teens in chat rooms. Quickly, the online discussions turned sexual. When the "girl" indicated she was home alone and interested in a date, eighteen men showed up at the house within a two-and-a-half-day period. These predators believed they were meeting a fourteen-year-old girl for sex. Instead, they found *Dateline*'s waiting cameras.

In addition to the *Dateline* sting, the media has covered numerous cases of adult men charged with sexually assaulting teenagers they met on MySpace. In one example, a Texas man was sentenced to seven years in jail for his plan to molest a fourteen-year-old girl he met on MySpace. The predator arrived to meet the girl with a hand-gun, rope restraints, condoms, and a digital camera. The "date" turned out to be an undercover investigator.

Why are predators searching online for victims? Because that is where the kids are. According to a Pew Internet & American Life Project survey, 49 percent of teens said they use social networking sites to make new friends. Looking for other teens, an unsuspecting victim may find a more dangerous friend. Parry Aftab, an Internet safety expert, noted that "pedophiles are using all of the social networking sites. And every other anonymous Internet technology to find kids. The social networking sites are where kids are."[26]

Despite the fear of predatory adults snatching unsuspecting teens, a recent study found that the majority of predators lure their victims willingly. Vulnerable teens who believe they are in love with the person they met online are most at risk for falling victim to a sexual predator.

Adult predators have honed the art of manipulating teens to gain their trust. They use information posted by the teens themselves to become closer to a potential victim. Teens do not always realize that anyone with Internet access can see their profile, posts, and pictures, including adult predators. According to Aftab, "If someone knows you . . . [extremely well] it's very easy online to be exactly what it is you're looking for—to be your 'soul mate.'"[27]

Some teens are watchful about strangers online. Caitlyn, a sixteen-year-old MySpace user, said: "There are a lot of creeps out there, and I know it. I don't let anybody add me to their friends list, and I don't accept messages from anybody I haven't met in person."[28] Unfortunately, other teens are not so savvy. They may turn down friend requests from strangers, but leave messages on public profiles about where and when they plan to meet up next. Any predator reading the open page knows exactly where to find them.

Janis Wolak conducted a study of sexual predators at the Crimes Against Children Research Center at the University of New Hampshire in Durham. She reported that "the great majority of cases we have seen involved young teenagers, mostly 13, 14, 15-year-old girls who are targeted by adults on the Internet who are straightforward about being interested in sex."[29]

Assistant State Attorney General Gene Fishel talks to high school students in Virginia about computer-based crimes. Law enforcement officials nationwide are stepping up efforts to keep people informed on issues of online safety and privacy protection.

The Figures on Stranger Danger

According to research by the Pew Internet & American Life Project, certain factors put teens at a higher risk of being contacted by a stranger. Girls, teens with social network profiles, and teens who post photos online are all more likely to be contacted by strangers who make them feel uncomfortable.

Teen categories	Percentage contacted by a stranger	Contacted by a stranger who made them feel uncomfortable or scared
All Teens	32 percent	7 percent
Boys	24	4
Girls	39	11
Teens with social network profiles	44	9
Teens without social network profiles	16	5
Teens who post photos online	49	10
Teens who do not post photos online	16	4

Aaron Smith, *Teens and Online Stranger Contact,* Pew Internet & American Life Project, October 14, 2007. www.pewinternet.org/pdfs/PIP_Stranger_Contact_Data_Memo.pdf.

In the study, researchers interviewed three thousand Internet users between the ages of ten and seventeen. According to study data, Internet predators used instant messages, e-mail, and chat rooms to meet victims. Once a potential victim was identified, the predator used these online tools to become close with the victim and establish a relationship. This grooming took place over a period of weeks or even months. According to Wolak, "From the perspective of the victim, these are romances."[30] Eventually, the victim, often believing he or she was in love, agreed to meet the predator in person.

STRANGER DANGER ONLINE

"The good news is that the vast majority of America's kids are much smarter and much more aware. . . . But the bad news is, there are a lot of [predators] out there who are still seeking, overwhelmingly for grooming and seduction. This remains a significant problem." —Ernie Allen, president of the National Center for Missing and Exploited Children.

Quoted in Janet Kornblum, "The Net Is a Circuit of Safety Concerns," *USA Today*, November 8, 2007.

Despite the risks, the study found most teens dealt with online strangers appropriately—blocking or ignoring them, leaving sites, or telling them to stop. According to a Pew Internet & American Life Project survey in 2006, 7 percent of online teens and 11 percent of online girls had been contacted online by a stranger who made them feel scared or uncomfortable. Teens with risky behavior, such as allowing strangers on buddy lists, talking about sex online with strangers, or being rude online, were more likely to attract predators. Wolak said: "One of the big factors we found is that offenders target kids who are willing to talk to them online. Most kids are not."[31]

Doing Drugs Online

The MySpace tagline is "a place for friends." The founders envisioned a place for people to gather around common interests and activities. But what if that common interest is drugs?

Sarah, a twelve-year-old from the Midwest, is an example of how social networking can feed and intensify a drug habit. When Sarah felt as if she did not fit in at school, she turned to MySpace and found a community of outsiders like herself. She experimented with drugs before going online, but her online contacts opened up a larger drug world to her. Online, she met drug dealers and other drug users. Several times, she arranged face-to-face meetings with her online contacts. She drifted further and further away from her family, even disappearing for days at a time. The easy access she found online fed her drug habit until she spiraled out of control. Finally, Sarah entered an intensive drug rehabilitation facility.

Because social networking sites are basically uncensored, they have become useful to teens looking to experiment with drugs. According to sixteen-year-old Edward, the "technology absolutely allows kids more access to drugs. There's no authority on the Internet, no one watches your every move, nobody is all up in your business." Edward himself used the Internet to order prescription drugs and have them sent to his house. Where did he find the doctors who provided the drugs? "Through friends I met on MySpace."[32]

Online, teens can explore drug culture. They can find ways to pass drug tests, post pictures of themselves or others getting high, and research drug recipes for making crack cocaine and LSD. Some teens like Sean use their profiles to display their drug activity. He says: "I had a MySpace profile. . . . Of course, everything that was in my profile was about getting high. My friends and I would post pictures from parties—one friend even had instructions on how to make drug paraphernalia."[33]

Even if a teen is not actively looking for drugs, his or her MySpace inbox may be flooded with spam from questionable online pharmacies. According to John Walters, director of the Office of National Drug Control Policy, "The pusher has moved to the PC; drug dealers lurk in these chat rooms just like pedophiles, targeting teens with pro-drug messages and offers of drugs."[34] These pushers might not even be adults, just other teens themselves.

Finding the drug culture online is not hard. Users decorate their profiles with marijuana leaves or colored pills in the wallpaper. Songs

Connections that teens make via online social networks are not always positive. Drug users, for example, can meet dealers and other users and find information that supports their habit.

with pro-drug lyrics are loaded to the profile. Many profiles also provide links to other pro-drug Web sites. Ahmanda, a sixteen-year-old on MySpace, explained how she attracted other drug users. "I . . . personalized my profile to attract other drug users or potential hookups; I have a large marijuana leaf as my background and pictures of me lighting a blunt [a joint]. In my 'About Me' section, I make it clear that I'm interested in drugs. I've had about fifty people request to be added and then want to get drugs from me."[35]

ON QUITTING A DRUG HABIT

"If it wasn't for MySpace, my parents' punishment could have worked. I could have been forced to stop using drugs. I could have lived on without ever having to be informed of the new E parties or raves; I could have stopped at fifteen. MySpace didn't let me." —Cherie, teenage drug addict.

Quoted in Candice M. Kelsey, *Generation MySpace: Helping Your Teen Survive Online Adolescence.* New York: Marlowe, 2007, p. 175.

In addition a number of drug groups exist on social networking sites. Teens looking for drug buddies can mingle online with other members of the group and exchange information. A recent search of MySpace found a group named National Pot Smokers. This public group was open to anyone to join as long as they smoked marijuana.

Online social networks do not make drug addicts. However, they do make it easy for teens to become more deeply involved in drug culture.

Porn in Social Networks

A quick search of several social network sites reveals the public profile of well-known porn star Jenna Jameson, a quiz titled "Are You Porn Star Material?" and a group called "I Want to Be a Porn Star." In years past, pornography stayed hidden in back rooms and stuffed under beds. Today pornography has become almost mainstream. Sexual images abound in advertising, television, and films. In fact, some people believe that society has begun to think of porn as a form of sexual expression.

Surrounded by sexual images and role models, it is not surprising that teens on social networking sites are mimicking the behavior they see—posting increasingly sexual photos and talking about sex all the time. Sex movies of celebrities such as Paris Hilton create a tremendous following when posted online.

This idolization of porn can be seen by some of the posts on adult film star Jenna Jameson's Facebook page. One teen writes in a post ". . . i want to be a pornstar when i graduate . . . . ive only got 4 more days!! then i begin trying to start my career as a pornstar."[36]

The porn industry has embraced social networks as a new marketing tool. Many adult film stars like Jameson have public pages on Facebook and MySpace. Anyone with Internet access can view their profiles and photos. In addition porn companies frequently set up profiles on social networks and send out friend requests to unsuspecting users. Often these profiles will include links to external and more graphic porn Web sites.

The official stance of social networks such as MySpace is that pornographic material has no place on their sites. In MySpace's official terms of use statement, content is banned if it "contains nudity, excessive violence or offensive subject matter or contains a link to an adult website."[37] According to Hemanshu Nigam, MySpace's head of security, his team "is looking at sites that go up, and identifying them. When somebody tells us about a site, we very quickly determine if our members rules are in violation or not, and then we take it down. And if there is any type of criminal activity, we report it to law enforcement."[38] Keeping up with the millions of sites, however, can prove to be a daunting task for the company's security team.

Who Is Keeping Teens Safe?

The dangers that teens encounter while using online social networks are real and significant. The combination of vulnerable teens and these adult threats can be a potentially lethal mix. But whose responsibility is social network safety? Is it the government's role to intervene and regulate these sites? Or should the sites themselves implement stricter guidelines and more effective policing? How should schools and parents educate teens about online safety? And what steps should teens themselves be taking to keep safe?

Starting at the Source: The Web Sites

Social networking sites have security teams and procedures designed to sift through activity on their site and flag any illegal or offensive material. Sites monitor user accounts and can remove content such as nudity that violates the user agreement. In reality, the sheer volume of sites to monitor allows many photos to slip past the safeguard and remain online for teens to view.

At a news conference in January 2008, Hemanshu Nigam, chief security officer for MySpace, speaks about his company's efforts to combat online sexual predators.

In response to a flurry of negative publicity linking the site to sexual predators, MySpace used a database of user information to identify and remove the profiles of sex offenders on its site. In July 2007 MySpace officials announced that over twenty-nine thousand profiles had been removed.

While officials acknowledge that dangerous activity does take place on social networking sites, they also stress that these dangers are in every community, online or not. Tom Anderson, cofounder of MySpace, believes that the negative activities happening on his site are nothing new. "Those things happen in any large community . . . the sense that MySpace is this place where all these bad things are happening is truly overblown."[39]

In 2008 over twenty high-tech businesses, including MySpace and Facebook, joined the Internet Safety Technical Task Force. The group's goal is to develop age and identity verification for online users. The social networking sites MySpace and Facebook also signed agreements with the attorneys general of forty-nine states and pledged to toughen safety measures online.

Should the Government Be Involved?

Pointing to the threat to children, several government officials and entities have gotten involved in the discussion about social networking safety.

Indiana enacted a new state law in 2008 that prohibits registered sex offenders who are convicted of crimes against children from using social networking sites. The law requires the offenders to turn over all e-mail addresses, passwords, and user names from any Internet provider to police. State officials plan to use this information to create sex offender databases.

At the federal level, Congress introduced the Deleting Online Predators Act in 2006. The act required schools to prevent students from accessing social networking sites and chat rooms unless doing it for an educational reason under the supervision of an adult. It also required public libraries to deny access to social networking sites to children, unless they had a parent's consent.

Several groups opposed the act. The American Library Association came out against the legislation. They claimed that the blanket blocking of sites as directed in the act would block access to some powerful learning applications. The users would no longer be able to take advantage of the full educational opportunities that the Internet offers.

Social networking researcher Danah Boyd warned against blocking teens' access to sites. "Blocking known sites will encourage teens to go further underground and seek out places to socialize that adults are unaware of," she said. "This puts youth at increased risk and means that neither educators nor law enforcement will be around to help."[40]

The act passed the House of Representatives in 2006 with an overwhelming majority in a 410 to 15 vote. But the act stalled in the Senate and was not signed into law.

Where Do Schools Fit In?

Many schools are uncertain where their responsibility falls when students go online. Some worry about the activities and sites that students access while on school property. But what about online activities when students are off campus?

Many schools have decided to deal with the safety issue by simply blocking access to social networking sites from school computers. But when the students go home, the issue becomes much grayer.

In Chicago a school district suspended three middle school students for posting obscene and threatening comments about a teacher on a blog. The school community was divided over the suspension. Some agreed with the school. Others thought the administrators had overstepped their authority. According to Steve Jones, a communications professor at the University of Illinois at Chicago: "It's an open question, because students have been writing these sorts of things for years but have been doing it in their notebooks, where nobody would have ever stumbled across it. With blogs, it's a sign of things to come—we're sort of testing the notions regarding free speech."[41]

Rather than blocking sites entirely, some experts recommend using schools to teach students about online safety. Who better to show young people the risks of online behavior and help them deal with risky situations? Educators can show teens how to use these sites in a controlled and supervised environment. Henry

Jenkins, the codirector of the Comparative Media Studies Program at MIT, commented, "Historically, we taught children what to do when a stranger telephoned them when their parents are away; surely, we should be helping to teach them how to manage the presentation of their selves in digital spaces."[42]

Parents and Teens: Safety Starts at Home

Given the risks facing teens online, it is not surprising that a number of parents have decided to ban social networking sites entirely from their homes. This approach, however, does not stop curious teens from accessing these sites from a friend's house and

Social Networking Safety Tips for Teens

According to Larry Magid and Anne Collier, authors of *MySpace Unraveled: A Parent's Guide to Teen Social Networking*, there are several safety precautions teens should follow online.

1. Be anonymous. Avoid posting information that would tell a stranger a physical location. That includes last names, school names, city names, local sports teams or hangout spots.

2. Set profiles to private. See what privacy features the site has and use them. Control access to profiles through a friends-only list. Be extremely selective in friends allowed on the list.

3. Don't meet with an online "friend." If there is a meeting, arrange it for a public place and bring friends.

4. Screen photos before posting. First, check for any identifying information. Is there a school name in the background? Overly sexual images can also be a source of unwanted attention. Remember that these photos can be downloaded and sent around the Internet.

5. Read between the "lines." People who are being overly nice may be more interested in manipulating than in friendship.

Larry Magid and Anne Collier, *MySpace Unraveled: A Parent's Guide to Teen Social Networking.* Berkeley, CA: Peachpit, 2007, p. 133.

Parents can promote Internet safety by closely monitoring their children's online activities and computer use.

creating profiles under a made-up name. Even worse, when these teens do run into trouble, they are less likely to report their problems to adults. They are afraid their Internet access will be cut off.

Some parents use filtering software to protect teens. These programs block children and teens from accessing inappropriate Web sites and content. The downside, however, is that these programs also block some useful sites like search engines. Liz Perle is the editor in chief of Common Sense Media, an organization that aims to improve the media life of kids and families. She disagrees with the use of filtering software. "Filters and blocking are absurd for teens," she says. "It's a fool's errand, and you might as well put your kid in a bag. You have to teach kids. They want to explore and see what's out there."[43]

PARENTS NEED TO SET SOCIAL NETWORKING RULES

"You're the parent. If you don't like it, unplug the computer. If they don't follow your rules, no Internet at all. If you're not the parent and if you're not going to step in, no Web site on earth is going to be able to help your child be safe." —Parry Aftab, Internet lawyer and safety expert.

Quoted in Rob Stafford, "Why Parents Must Mind MySpace," MSNBC.com, April 5, 2006. www.msnbc.msn.com/id/11064451.

Most experts do recommend that parents stay involved in their child's online life. Steps such as monitoring online activity and checking in on the teen's profile and their friends' profiles can alert parents if teens are straying into dangerous territory. Also, parents should keep the family computer in a public space to make it difficult for users to hide the sites they visit. Simple online searches of a teen's name and information can alert parents to any unknown blogs or profiles.

While parents and other groups work to increase the safety of online networks, teens and other users are ultimately responsible for their own actions on these sites. Several simple steps such as limiting profiles to friends only and using password protection features can keep out unwanted attention. Other important steps include keeping personal information private and taking any discussion of sexual and emotional issues off the Web. Users should also evaluate the benefit and risk of participating in online groups and forums.

Despite the risks online, smart and savvy use of social networking sites can be a safe experience. It can also be a bonding experience for the family. According to Anne Collier, editor of *NetFamilyNews*: "The Internet presents a remarkable opportunity to parents and kids for a kind of partnership. Kids can teach their parents about the technology, while parents can teach their kids internet street smarts."[44]

THE BLURRED LINE BETWEEN PRIVATE AND PUBLIC LIVES

One of the biggest decisions any social network user faces is how much information to share in his or her profile. Many social network users feel a false sense of security on their site. This can affect their decision-making process. For teens with a public profile, most of what is posted on social networks can be viewed by anyone. Teens may post pictures and text for friends to see, but their posts are read by parents, teachers, college officials, and employers. Stalkers and pedophiles may also be logged on, reading a teen's site and trying to make contact.

So What Are Teens Posting?

"Not long ago, young people would die at the prospect of their mother or their friend discovering their diaries," said Rochelle Gurstein, author of *The Repeal of Reticence*, which details the erosion of privacy in the United States. "The teenage girl that used to be the most vulnerable, protected member of society is now unsupervised, left to her own devices, with access to the Internet, and what does she do? Broadcasts to the whole world to see her in her most vulnerable moments."[45]

Today's teens have been raised in a digital world. Using online networks to express their thoughts and feelings is a natural extension. Sixteen-year-old Emily turned online after her mother found her paper diary. "When there were days when I just needed to rant, it felt good. I'd come home after school, and I'd spend, like, an hour typing in everything I did all day." Emily started a blog on the social networking site Xanga. "Once I discovered, like, posting online, it definitely became, 'Why would I write it in a book?'"[46]

The teen tradition of capturing private thoughts and feelings in a diary has given way to blogging in the digital age.

What Teens Post Online

According to the 2007 Pew Internet & American Life Project study *Teens, Privacy & Online Social Networks*, teens post a variety of personal information on their social network profiles.

First name—82 percent
Photos of themselves—79 percent
Photos of friends—66 percent
Name of city or town—
   61 percent
Name of school—49 percent

Instant message screen name—
   40 percent
Streamed audio—40 percent
Links to their blog—39 percent
E-mail address—29 percent
Last name—29 percent
Videos—29 percent
Cell phone number—2 percent

Amanda Lenhart and Mary Madden, *Teens, Privacy & Online Social Networks.* Pew Internet & American Life Project, April 18, 2007, p. ii. www.pewinternet.org/pdfs/PIP_Teens_Privacy_SNS_Report_Final.pdf.

Online diaries can be made "secret blogs" that only the writer can read. Users can decide to open up their online diaries to a select list of friends. Many, however, choose to allow open access, inviting the world to read. Jeremy, a Virginia Tech graduate who has a LiveJournal diary, explained: "Everything everyone's writing online, they want it there because they want it to be read by someone. . . . Having someone read your secret feels better."[47]

Parents, teachers, and law enforcement officers, however, feel less enthusiastic about posting details of private lives online. Jeremy's mother, Karen, was horrified when she discovered her children kept online diaries. "I just thought it was terrible, horrible. I just couldn't imagine why you would put your feelings and personal comments on something that just went out there."[48]

Making Privacy Decisions

While teens are posting more personal content online, a 2007 study by the Pew Internet & American Life Project found that most teens are aware of privacy concerns and do take some steps to protect themselves online. They make decisions as to which information should be restricted to friends and what should be posted for a broader audience. The study found that 66 percent of teens with an online profile restrict it in some way. Restrictions could be in the form of making profiles private, using a password protection feature, hiding profiles, or taking them offline entirely.

How much teens decide to share varies from person to person. The user's age and gender frequently play a role in privacy decisions.

As the Pew study found, the most common thing for teens to post on their site is their first name (82%), followed closely by photos of themselves (79%). Other information that is common to find is the names of their town and school, instant message name, e-mail address, and even last names. A few teens (2%) will even post their cell phone numbers.

Girls and boys approach privacy differently. The Pew study found that girls are more concerned with not posting information that could lead to finding their physical location. In a focus group, one high school girl talked about how she decides what to post on her profile.

> I try to post as little information as possible. There is no way of knowing who is going to see the information posted and I'm really stingy. I don't think it's okay to share last names, date of birth, where I live, anything that will help people identify me. Pictures are OK because it's really difficult to find someone if the only thing you know about them is what they look like.[49]

On the other hand, boys are more likely to post how to reach them—where they live, last names, and even cell phone numbers.

The Pew study found that older teens aged fifteen to seventeen are more likely than younger teens to post personal information on public profiles. Older teens commonly share photos of themselves and friends on their sites. They are also more likely to disclose their school name.

For teens that do decide to share some or all of their profile with the public, 56 percent give some false information in the profile. One middle school girl talked about why she posted fake facts: "I don't want anyone to know where I'm from. You don't need the people that you know to be able to read where you're

Teens often limit the amount of personal information they provide in their online profiles and sometimes post false information in order to protect their privacy.

from because they already know."[50] Other teens use fake information for different reasons. One high school boy talked about his fake profile. "I use a pseudonym, who is 24. Because I regard myself as an intellectual, it's easier to be taken seriously if people don't know they're talking to a sixteen-year-old. You'd be surprised what respect eight years buys you."[51]

Users who are diligent in keeping profiles and pictures free of personal information may slip when chatting with friends or posting on a friend's site. An online conversation that gives the time and place friends plan to meet may reveal more information than intended. While feeling secure in the context of an online conversation, users may reveal details about class schedules and other personal facts. But the truth is anyone could be reading those posts.

Some teens, however, believe the fuss about online privacy is overblown. Tyler, a high school freshman, thinks that keeping personal information out of social networking defeats its purpose. "I know how annoying it is to look for people and it being impossible to find them," he says. Tyler lists his high school name on his profile so that friends can more easily find him. He does acknowledge that keeping personal information public has its risks. "But I'm not going to be stupid about it," he says. "We all get messages from weird old men who are like 'hi'—but nobody replies to them."[52]

Privacy Leaks

Even users who restrict access to their profile may be vulnerable to privacy risks. Sarah, an education major at St. Joseph College, locks down the information on her Facebook profile routinely. She says: "I don't want to have to worry about all the different online scandals and problems. It's just common sense."[53] However, even users like Sarah share private information every time they download and install an application on their site.

Applications, also known as widgets, are mini-programs that allow users to personalize their page. They may be silly games, trivia quizzes, or daily horoscopes. Most of these applications require users to give access to personal information in order to load them on a profile. "You want to be social with your friends, but now you're giving 20 guys you've never met vast amounts of information from your profile," warned Chris Soghoian, a cybersecurity researcher at Indiana University. "That should be troubling to people."[54]

Think Before Posting Online

"In the beginning, I kind of posted whatever without really thinking about it. I could have saved myself a lot of misery had I just
sat down and used my common sense." —Michael Guinn, college student expelled for content on Facebook profile.

Quoted in Janet Kornblum and Mary Beth Marklein, "What You Say Online Could Haunt
You," *USA Today*, March 8, 2006. www.usatoday.com/tech/news/internetprivacy/2006-
03-08-facebook-myspace_x.htm.

Facebook and MySpace, two sites that offer applications, in-
sist that their application developers must follow strict policies
and standards that limit what they can do with user information.
But most security experts agree that access to too much personal
information is not a good thing. "I suspect that there's a whole lot
of clicking without a lot of thinking," said Mary Madden, a senior
researcher at the Pew Internet & American Life Project. "So much
of this sharing happens in a way that users don't see the consequences. It's kind of a big, black hole."[55]

Who Is Reading Social Network Sites?

As noted in the Pew study, most users are at least thinking about
privacy decisions and taking steps to protect themselves from
strangers online. But what happens when the person reading a
profile is not a stranger? As the popularity of social networks continues to grow, users find themselves online with more than just
a circle of friends. Suddenly, parents, teachers, university admission officers, and future employers are online and reading user
profiles.

One of the biggest risks for social network users is posting
content without thinking about who exactly will be reading it.
What seems like a funny picture to share with friends may not be
so impressive to a teacher or college admissions counselor. According to child psychologist David Welsh, "Most of the situations I'm running across in my practice are kids being caught by
surprise, sort of, at how incredibly public and accessible (the
blogs are)." He believes that user names instead of real names can

lead to a false sense of security. He says, "It's an odd mix of a perceived anonymity with an obviously very public forum."[56]

Friending Mom and Dad

As more parents ask to "friend" their teen online, teens may struggle with separating the content intended for friends from what they want to share with other adults, including their parents. As parents go online, they may not like what they see. "It blew me away," said Marcy, mother of a thirteen-year-old, when she read her daughter's profile. "And I just lost it."[57]

Some teens design their sites knowing that parents may be watching. One high school girl in the Pew study talked about what content she posts in a growing public environment. "Like if my Mom saw it I wouldn't care. I'm really careful with that whole MySpace thing. I've heard of employers not hiring people because of it. So I just put things up there that if my Grandma or Mom saw it I wouldn't care. It wouldn't be a big deal."[58] A middle school girl agreed, "When I'm on MySpace I will never put anything on it that I wouldn't want my parents to see."[59]

Teachers Read Profiles, Too

In addition to parents, teachers and schools are getting involved with social networks. Where the school's responsibility lies is a blurry line. Do they have a right to monitor students' online activities after school and off campus? Or is too much involvement a violation of students' right to privacy?

Some schools draw the line when social network activity begins to affect the school and other students. In Costa Mesa, California, a middle school expelled a student for posting threats against a classmate. In addition twenty of his classmates also received suspensions for viewing the posts.

"We are trying to figure out how our school rules relate to this type of behavior,"[60] said Meredyth Cole, the assistant head of the Madeira School in the Washington, D.C., area. She decided to send a letter to the parents of her private school students, warning them about students' use of social networking sites. In New Jersey, a Catholic school decided to ban the use of social networking sites by its students, even at home. Experts

Some parents are shocked by the postings their children make on social networking sites.

debate whether this ban is legal or a violation of the students' free speech rights.

SOCIAL NETWORKING SITES SHOULD NOT BE CENSORED

"The best way to counter bad speech is with good speech, not with suspensions and censorship. . . . School officials should be extremely cautious before attempting to limit student expression on a private Web site maintained off school grounds." —Sam Chaltain, director of the First Amendment Schools Project.

Quoted in Paula Reed Ward, "Schools Perceive Threat to Authority in Student Internet Postings," *Pittsburgh Post-Gazette*, February 5, 2006.

Tim Trautman, head of the Barrie School in Silver Spring, Maryland, explained his school's policy. "We try . . . to say that the boundaries are on school grounds and within school time, but if there is a case that does tend to spill over and directly impact campus life, all of a sudden space and location, the geography of it, becomes less important."[61]

College Officials Are Watching

Even college students feel the impact of their social network activities reaching an unintended audience. Michael, a student at John Brown University, a Christian college in Arkansas, posted pictures of himself dressed in drag on his Facebook site. It started as a funny joke for friends. But things turned serious when university administrators logged on and viewed his site, which also included discussions of his gay lifestyle. Michael was kicked out of school. Administrators cited the postings on his site as clear evidence that he had violated campus conduct codes that behavior must follow guidelines found in Scripture.

A twenty-year-old student at Iowa Western Community College wrote an entry on his site that some people in his dorm should be shot. When college officials learned of the entry and other threatening posts, they expelled him and banned him from campus. Despite the student's protests that the posts were meaningless and the punishment excessive, the damage was done.

Other students have been suspended or expelled when colleges discover pictures of them drinking underage or posing with drug paraphernalia. But are these punishments appropriate? "As more students are suspended and disciplined, we're going to need some clear guidance from the courts," urged David Hudson Jr., an attorney at the First Amendment Center in Nashville. "Right now, it is not clear just how far the authority of school officials extends."[62]

Layshock v. Hermitage School District

In 2007 a federal court ruled the Hermitage School District in Pennsylvania violated the First Amendment free-speech rights of student Justin Layshock for punishing him for a profile he created on MySpace.

The controversy started in 2005 when Justin, along with several friends, posted parodies of his principal on MySpace. The profiles made fun of the principal and used profanity. Justin created his profile outside of school hours and off school property. When school administrators discovered the MySpace profiles, they spent a large amount of time investigating to find the creators.

When administrators identified Justin as one of the Web page creators, the school punished him with a ten-day out-of-school suspension. They removed him from honors classes and placed him in an alternative curriculum education program for the remaining school year.

The ACLU of Pennsylvania filed the lawsuit on Justin's behalf. They claimed the school district's punishment for off-campus speech violated Justin's First Amendment free-speech rights.

The court agreed. "The mere fact that the internet may be accessed at school does not authorize school officials to become censors of the world-wide web," said U.S. District Judge Terrence McVerry. "Public schools are vital institutions but their reach is not unlimited."

Quoted in American Civil Liberties Union of Pennsylvania, "Judge Finds Suspension of Student for MySpace Parody of School Principal Unconstitutional," July 11, 2007.

MORE THAN FRIENDS ARE WATCHING

"Just some of the pictures I ran across [on Facebook]—I couldn't believe it. . . . You can only think: What if one of the big accounting firms comes across this, or a law firm or law school or graduate school?" —Cheryl Barnard, associate dean of student affairs at Quinnipiac University in Hamden, Connecticut.

Quoted in Janet Kornblum and Mary Beth Marklein, "What You Say Online Could Haunt You," *USA Today*, March 8, 2006. www.usatoday.com/tech/news/internetprivacy/2006-03-08-facebook-myspace_x.htm.

In addition to teachers and school administrators, the college admissions office is getting involved in social networks. At Reed College in Portland, Oregon, admissions dean Paul Marthers admits that his department will review an applicant's profile. In one case, Reed denied admission to an applicant who bragged of plans to beat Reed's financial aid system and posted hostile messages about some Reed officials. "How could we not factor in the life he was having on LiveJournal?"[63] asked Marthers.

Hiring Decisions

Employers consider online profiles when evaluating job candidates. In one example, the president of a small consulting company in Chicago decided to check on a potential intern. On the candidate's Facebook page, the executive found descriptions of marijuana, shooting people, and obsessive sex. Whether the content was truthful or just exaggeration did not matter. It landed the job seeker in the rejection pile. "A lot of it makes me think, what kind of judgment does this person have?" said Brad Karsh, the company's president. "Why are you allowing this to be viewed publicly, effectively, or semipublicly?"[64]

Karsh's company is not alone. A survey of employers in the University of Dayton career counselor database found that 42 percent said they would consider an online profile in their hiring decision. According to Michael Sciola, director of the career resource center at Wesleyan University: "It's a growing phenomenon. There are lots of employers that Google. Now they've taken the next

In addition to reviewing résumés and conducting interviews, some employers also research job candidates' online profiles in order to help them make hiring decisions.

step."[65] Trudy Steinfeld, executive director of the Center for Career Development at New York University, agrees. She says: "The term they've used over and over is red flags. Is there something about their lifestyle that we might find questionable or that we might find goes against the core values of our corporation?"[66]

Other companies such as Enterprise Rent-a-Car and Osram Sylvania purposely choose not to explore applicants' online lives. "I'd rather not see that part of them," said Maureen Crawford Hentz, manager of talent acquisition at Osram Sylvania. "I don't think it's related to their bona fide occupational qualifications."[67]

Career counselors at many colleges have counseled students to review their social network sites. They caution students to remove anything inappropriate for an audience of employers and other adults. But whether or not the advice is being heard is unknown. "I think students have the view that Facebook is their space and that the adult world doesn't know about it," said Mark W. Smith, assistant vice chancellor and director of the career center at Washington University in St. Louis. "But the adult world is starting to come in."[68]

Professional Versus Personal Lives

Even for adults, the mixing of public and private worlds online can cause problems. For some users, requests from professional contacts to friend online can be tricky. Andrew Ledbetter, an assistant professor of communications studies at Ohio University in Athens, noted, "On Facebook, my high school pals, college buddies and grad school friends are lumped together with former students, current students and professional colleagues, in one big social group."[69] Ledbetter admits that he has decided not to post certain content because he believes it would not be appropriate for all of the groups in his online network.

Other users juggle the personal versus public debate by making their profiles specific to only one audience. Chuck Sanchez deleted mention of his public relations firm on his MySpace page. He explains: "It's simply not worth it. I want my personal site to be just that: personal."[70]

Teacher Ardath Steward uses her site to keep in touch with family. But she has also made sure the content is appropriate for her middle school students to see. "There's no risky content on mine for a reason," she says. "WWW means anyone can see what you do. Why would I want to jeopardize my professional career?"[71]

The Long Life of Web Content

Unfortunately, cleaning up a social network profile is not as easy at it sounds. Once a photo, blog entry, or instant message hits online, users lose control. It can be printed, uploaded to other online sites, and passed around in e-mail or instant messaging chains. Users cannot take it back. Suddenly, that unflattering picture is moving around the Internet indefinitely. According to Larry Rosen, a psychology professor at California State University at Dominguez Hills, users who believe they have taken the right

People may find themselves haunted for years by embarrassing images and postings they thought they had deleted.

steps to keep information private may be wrong. "It's public, whether they like it or not," he says. "And they think they can delete things, but anyone could have copied it and pasted it."[72]

Even if content is not hijacked by other users, a permanent Internet library may allow it to live on forever. A group called the Internet Archive saves almost everything on the Web. According to their site, they are building a library of digital sites with free access to the general public. Content can also slip out of control on search engines like Google that save changed or deleted Web pages.

As online social networks become more embedded in our society, the rules about privacy will continue to evolve. According to Danah Boyd, social networking expert at the University of California at Berkeley, young people growing up in an online world no longer see privacy as keeping information confined to oneself. Instead, it has become a matter of controlling who has access. Boyd says, "Information is not private because no one knows it; it is private because the knowing is limited and controlled."[73]

THE THREAT
OF CYBERTERRORISM

Online social networking connects people from different backgrounds and countries. Unfortunately, what began as a place to share information and socialize also offers a place for terrorists and other extremists to conduct a new type of warfare—cyberterrorism.

The Evolution of Cyberterrorism

According to the National Conference of State Legislatures, cyberterrorism is "the use of information technology by terrorist groups and individuals to further their agenda."[74] Cyberterrorism includes hacking into computer systems, spreading viruses, bringing Web sites offline, or making online threats. With the rise of online social networking, terrorists have expanded their presence. They have become active in forums, social networks, chat rooms, and Web sites.

IT ONLY TAKES ONE

"The challenge cyber-terrorism poses is that you don't even need to be a group to commit cyber-terrorism. A 16-year-old kid on the other side of the world . . . can do the type of damage it used to take armies to do." —Michael Chertoff, former secretary of the Department of Homeland Security.

Quoted in John Wildermuth, "Cyber-Threat Rising, Chertoff Says. Homeland Security Boss Speaks to Group in Silicon Valley," *San Francisco Chronicle*, July 29, 2005.

Prior to the spread of the Internet in the 1990s, terrorists worked through centralized groups such as al Qaeda. These groups

Malika El Aroud: Internet Warrior

A middle-aged woman types at a computer in her three-room apartment in Brussels. Draped in a traditional Islamic black veil, Malika El Aroud does not look like a famous Internet jihadist. Yet, writing under the name "Oum Obeyda," she has become a "female holy warrior" for al Qaeda. In chat rooms and forums, El Aroud spreads her hatred of the West. From her computer keyboard, she prods Muslim men to fight and Muslim women to join her in support of their cause. "It's not my role to set off bombs," she says. "I have a weapon. It's to write. It's to speak out. That's my jihad. You can do many things with words. Writing is also a bomb."

Under constant surveillance, El Aroud is well-known by European intelligence officials. Even though she is not part of any terrorist operations, she still poses a threat. According to Claude Moniquet, president of the European Strategic Intelligence and Security Center in Brussels: "Malika is a role model, an icon who is bold enough to identify herself. She plays a very important strategic role as a

In June 2007, Malika El Aroud and her husband, Moez Garsallaoui, walk into a Swiss courtroom to begin their trial on charges of running Web sites advocating and promoting terrorist acts.

source of inspiration. She's very clever—and extremely dangerous."

Quoted in Elaine Sciolino and Souad Mekhennet, "Al Qaeda Warrior Uses Internet to Rally Women," *New York Times*, May 28, 2008.

organized and mobilized attacks. After the 9/11 disaster, the United States declared a war on terror. It destroyed many terrorist camps and central command units in Afghanistan and Iraq. Unable to reform traditional groups, terrorists turned to the Internet as a new network for communicating, recruiting, and planning attacks.

The Internet has allowed terrorists to break through geographical and cultural barriers. It enables terrorists to form a global community that reaches across nationality, age, and gender. Groups spread around the world share ideology and strategy, generating a feeling of community.

A 2001 Department of Defense surveillance image shows a terrorist training camp in Afghanistan before it was destroyed in an air strike by U.S. and British warplanes. Terrorists now use the Internet to congregate, recruit, and plan attacks.

GARMABAK GHAR TERRORIST TRAINING CAMP, AFGHANISTAN

PRE STRIKE

According to Brian Michael Jenkins, a transportation security expert, the power of the Internet enables terrorist groups to accomplish more damage with fewer resources. "The power to kill, destroy and disrupt is descending into the hands of smaller and smaller groups," he says. "The fanatics and lunatics who have existed through history are becoming an even more imposing force."[75] No longer are large groups of extremists needed. Now only one person at a keyboard can do a significant amount of damage.

Is Cyberterrorism a Real Threat?

Some experts do not see cyberterrorism as a real threat. They doubt that cyber attacks could cause the same amount of destruction as traditional physical attacks. They believe that concern over possible nuclear meltdowns and chemical plant explosions is exaggerated. According to Stephen Cummings, director of the British government's Centre for the Protection of National Infrastructure, "The discussion of cyberterrorism distracts our attention from the more pressing terrorist threats, which are still physical."[76]

Others point out the potential combination of physical and cyber attacks. Disrupting power supply or communications during an attack could lead to greater destruction, confusion, and terror.

Infrastructure Attacks

Years ago, engineers designed the control systems for hundreds of utilities, chemical factories, and other U.S. critical systems when each was a stand-alone entity. Now many of these utilities connect online for remote monitoring and instant communications. Without changes to older control systems, these entities are an easy target for cyber attacks.

Cyber experts claim terrorists could shut down parts of the Internet, phone systems, and electric grids by simply hacking into poorly defended computer systems. "I could easily turn off the power in a couple dozen cities,"[77] said Jason Larsen, a computer programmer at the Idaho National Engineering and Environmental Laboratory. Getting into automated control systems at several big utilities took him a week. Other vulnerable targets

U.S. security experts have made efforts to monitor and upgrade the computer networks that run power plants and other aspects of the nation's infrastructure in order to minimize their vulnerability to cyberterrorist hackers.

include military communication systems, dam floodgates, and air traffic control systems.

Terrorist groups have recognized the weakness. Keith Lordeau, an FBI assistant director, told the U.S. Senate that "terrorist groups have shown a clear interest in developing basic hacking tools, and the FBI predicts that terrorist groups will either develop or hire hackers."[78] Beyond terrorist groups, intelligence agencies suspect that foreign governments such as Iran, North Korea, Russia, and China have already trained hackers for computer warfare.

Electronic Jihad

Not only are terrorists using the Internet to attack infrastructure targets, they are also organizing attacks online. Electronic jihad is a type of cyberterrorism that attempts to cause network and economic disruption. According to Dorothy Denning, a professor in the Department of Defense Analysis at the Naval Postgraduate School, "The attacks from jihadists are interested in taking Web sites down and destroying economies that they don't like. It's something to be taken seriously."[79]

Electronic jihad relies primarily on denial of service attacks. During such an attack, the terrorists flood a target site with so many requests for information that the site crashes. One such attack took place in the country of Estonia in the spring of 2007. Hackers shut down numerous Web sites and changed the pages of others.

No group has officially claimed responsibility for the Estonian attacks. Many people suspect that a feud with Russia over the relocation of a Soviet war monument sparked the cyber attack. Estonia's president, Toomas Hendrik, said in a press conference: "When you are a highly Interneted country like we are, then these kinds of attacks can do very serious damage. And I do think it's the wave of the future—not that it's a good wave, but it is something that we have to deal with more and more."[80]

Web Sites for Terror Groups

While experts debate the seriousness of threats to infrastructure and cyber assets, terrorists continue to use the Internet every day. The features that made the Internet an invaluable tool in everyday life benefit terrorist groups as well. Communication is fast, anonymous, and subject to very little regulation or governmental control. There is easy and inexpensive access to tremendous numbers of people. Users can spread their message with text, graphics, audio, and video.

Virtually all active terrorist groups have stepped onto the Internet. Most of them have Web sites, sometimes more than one and in several languages. These groups are global, including Hamas in the Middle East, the Irish Republican Army, Peru's Tupak-Amaru, and the Japanese Red Army.

Despite the differences in background, culture, and political ideology, terrorist sites generally follow a similar format. The site usually has a history of the organization and biographies of its leaders and heroes. The site also explains the group's political goals and criticizes its enemies. Current news and details about the group's latest activities are also often included on the site.

Mention of the group's violent actions and any consequences is frequently missing from Web sites. This helps to build a positive image with potential supporters. The groups Hizballah and Hamas do not follow this pattern, however. To date, they have chosen to update their Web sites with details of daily operations. They display the total number of enemies killed and soldiers or "martyrs" sacrificed.

Online Networking Opens Doors

Beyond Web sites, the growth of online social networking has put more tools into the hands of terrorists. Password-protected message boards and forums are a popular form of communication and networking for online terrorists. Within forums, individual members can learn, share information, and network with each other. Members of terror groups are also using e-mail, blogs, instant messaging, and social networks to promote their agenda. Social networks and their tools allow terrorist groups to gain support from sympathizers, promote terrorism, and recruit new members from around the world.

Publicity and Propaganda

The Internet has given terrorist groups an expanded opportunity for publicity. They are no longer dependent on traditional media to draw attention to their cause. The ability to control and upload their own content allows these groups to decide what message to send and when to deliver it. They choose how to portray themselves, their goals, and their enemies.

The freedom to upload content gives terrorist groups a perfect platform to spread propaganda. They highlight perceived restrictions on their freedoms and the suffering of sympathetic political prisoners. The groups post arguments on the Web sites to justify their use of violence. Often, they try to present themselves as a persecuted people, standing up against oppression. Uploaded videos and links to other sympathetic Web sites help these groups continue their efforts to promote terrorism.

Some groups spread fear and threats online, a type of psychological warfare. Videotapes of murders, such as that of American journalist Daniel Pearl, played on several terrorist Web sites. The Internet's uncensored nature allows organizations to post these threatening messages as a warning to their enemies.

Recruiting and Networking

Social networking sites provide an interactive place for terrorist groups to recruit supporters. Features of these sites such as chat rooms and bulletin boards can be used actively to hunt down recruits. Once identified, the recruits can receive access into password-protected forums and message boards. Often they also gain access to propaganda materials and terrorist training manuals.

The Islamic Army in Iraq's Web site is one example of terrorists on the Web. Their site features videos of attacks, pictures of dead U.S. soldiers, and an English translation of al Qaeda communications. According to Rita Katz, director of the SITE Institute in Washington, D.C.: "We know for sure the al-Qaeda is trying to recruit as many as possible from the Western societies, not people who look like Arabs. This is a good place to be if you want to recruit people like that."[81]

Young people are often the target for recruiters. Their impressionable nature makes them more receptive to the terrorist message. Jerrold Post is director of the political psychology program at George Washington University. He believes these sites are creating "a virtual community of hatred and seeding these ideas very early."[82]

Spanish police guard a suspect arrested in 2007 for using the Internet to recruit other fighters to plan and carry out terrorist attacks.

Terrorists from different groups and countries mingle together on social networking sites. Together, organizations share information about tactics and weapons. They swap specific suggestions on bomb making and organizing attacks. The ease of communication allows these groups to become more decentralized. As a result, terrorist communications have become faster and cheaper than ever.

Planning an Attack

The World Wide Web offers a treasure trove of information for terrorists to use. Multiple sites offer how-to instructions for building bombs and chemical weapons. Handbooks detail the use of poisons and how to plan attacks.

Terrorist groups also rely on the Internet as they plan attacks. When federal officials arrested al Qaeda terrorist Abu Zubayda in connection with the 9/11 attacks, they found thousands of encrypted messages in a password-protected area of a Web site. Hamas uses chat rooms to send e-mail, plan operations, and coordinate actions. Coded messages disguise important information such as maps and instructions.

Popular forums are full of messages about weapons of mass destruction. In one example, a member of a password-protected forum discussed a potential attack on Texas Stadium. He explained the attack plan and posted pictures of the stadium and explosives. He said: "One of the suiciders will execute the explosions in one of the stadium corners. When the people are

View of a Cyber Attack

In June 2003 extremist Abr Aheem posted a message on a Web site. He announced that the Electronic Al-Qasam Brigade was ready to launch an attack. A fellow extremist replied that three thousand were ready to join in the attack. The pair posted instructions for the planned denial-of-service attack on a Web site for followers to read. They planned to take down several Israeli Web sites in four days.

Unknown to the terrorists, cyber spies at IDefense, a security intelligence firm based in Virginia, were reading the posts. Fluent in Arabic, they warned the Israeli targets about the plot before the attack. When the jihadists launched their assault against a list of target Web sites, the Web sites stayed functional. The attack failed.

Despite the failure, the terrorists regrouped to learn from their mistakes and begin planning their next assault. In one message, they said, "God willing our next attack will have better performance on our side."

Quoted in Nathan Vardi, "Jihadists@Work," *Forbes*, September 20, 2004.

rushing and dashing to flee, another brother will explode himself at one of the gates . . . the goal is not to kill hundreds only. This goal is to kill thousands."[83] While this specific plan was unsuccessful, it demonstrates the chilling intent recorded on these sites.

Once an idea lands online, it becomes part of the terrorist community, regardless of whether the original planner is still able to execute the idea. Any member of the group can step in to the plan and continue marching toward the target.

Efforts to Counter Cyberterrorism

Governments and law enforcement agencies are distinctly aware of the threat of cyberterrorism. Before the Iraq war, online jihad was simply a handful of open chat rooms where members could vent their anger. With social networking's global connections, the terrorist groups have evolved into a more decentralized structure. In addition the terrorists have become smarter about security and keeping their identity secret. These changes have made tracking and stopping terrorists even more difficult.

TERRORISTS ON THE INTERNET

"Since the events of 9/11, terrorist presence online has multiplied tenfold. Around the year 2000, there were 70 to 80 core terrorist sites online; now there are at least 7,000 to 8,000." —Hsinchun Chen, director of the University of Arizona's Artificial Intelligence Lab.

Quoted in Steven Kotler, "'Dark Web' Project Takes on Cyber-Terrorism," FoxNews.com, October 12, 2007. www.foxnews.com/story/0,2933,300956,00.html.

Since 9/11, law enforcement has identified specific Web sites that they believe are linked to terrorist groups such as al Qaeda. These sites often have some form of attack planning, from threats to directions for supporters. Once identified, agents monitor these sites for clues about terrorist activity.

Law enforcement uses the same online tools such as forums and chat rooms to track terrorists and monitor their activities.

U.S. law enforcement officials monitor chat rooms, forums, and Web sites, such as this site backed by an Asian militant group that advocates terrorism, in order to track the activities of terrorist groups.

According to Ned Moran, an intelligence analyst with the Terrorism Research Center: "The Internet is a double-edged sword. Al-Qaeda uses the Internet as a meeting point, a proving ground, a place to recruit from, and there is a lot of concern about that. But it also makes them vulnerable because we can track their postings and disrupt them."[84]

Agencies monitor suspected terrorist sites for clues to impending attacks. They also follow links to other wanted criminals. To get into a password-protected forum, an undercover agent will assume a fake identity. Once granted access to the forum, the agent works to gain the other members' trust. Once inside, agents track chat room discussions and record information about activities.

The hard part about monitoring online terrorists is deciding which posts are legitimate. Evan Kohlmann, a terrorism consultant from Seattle, talked about the difficulty in identifying potential threats. "You get one out of 50 that are capable and smart and have resources on the ground. And there's no telling what kind of a catastrophic event that they can pull off."[85]

Unfortunately, the increasing number of terrorist Web sites, message boards, and chat rooms makes it nearly impossible for law enforcement to monitor each one. In 1998 Gabriel Weimann, author of the book *Terror on the Internet*, monitored approximately twelve terrorist Web sites. In 2008 he watched fifty-five hundred.

To help, terrorist watch groups have developed tools to sift through mountains of Web information. Researchers from the Artificial Intelligence Lab at the University of Arizona created a system named the Dark Web. The Dark Web is a series of automated tools that collect and analyze terrorist content on the Internet. Hsinchun Chen, director of the Artificial Intelligence Lab, described the purpose of Dark Web: "It's really trying to collect all the terrorist generated content in the world, and when I say 'all' I mean from websites to forums to chat rooms to blogs to videos to voice recordings and so on, everything they produce. We really want to learn directly from them what are they thinking and what are their strategy, ideology, propagandas and so on."[86]

The Dark Web enables watchers to sort through information quickly. "Some forums have a quarter million people posting, so there is no way anyone can eyeball those results. We can analyse millions of postings in a matter of seconds,"[87] said Chen.

Along with other analytical tools, the Dark Web uses sentiment and social-network analysis. Sentiment analysis looks for hate and rage emotions to identify more serious threats. Social-network analysis maps extremist networks. It works to identify each member's place in the network and his or her level of importance.

AWARENESS OF CYBER THREATS

"The one thing that I worry about is lack of awareness. I think that will be one of our biggest challenges . . . how important everybody's role is, that one computer . . . can be the portal through which an attack is launched." —Gregory Garcia, first assistant secretary for cybersecurity and telecommunications at the Homeland Security Department.

Quoted in Patience Wait, "Defense Domain, Civilian Awareness: Elder, Garcia Walk Two Sides of the Cybersecurity Beat," *Government Computer News*, January 22, 2007.

Even with improved computer tools, human judgment is still important to track online terrorists and determine which content should be taken seriously. According to Weimann: "What automated search can do is save expenses, manpower and time. But it is limited in the depth of the analysis. Human eyes and mind see more and deeper than a crawler."[88]

To Shut Down or Not?

The debate rages about what to do with online sites that display terrorist threats and plots. Some people believe authorities should shut down these problem sites. The absence of the sites will make communications more difficult for the terrorists. Critics contend that the fluid nature of the Internet makes this approach useless. They believe a shut-down site may reappear under a new name and Web address, but still promote the same ideals and content.

Other people claim that watching terrorist sites gives valuable intelligence to law enforcement. Keeping sites open allows agents better to understand how terrorists work and evolve on the Internet. In this case, the focus should be on developing better ways to monitor terrorist activities, not shutting down sites

What responsibility do the social networking sites have to monitor terrorist content? It is a difficult question to answer. According to Paul McMasters, a free speech expert at the Freedom Forum: "It is a very fine line to walk sometimes. But our tradition under the First Amendment is always: Come down on the side of more speech, not less speech."[89] Bruce Hoffman, director of the RAND Institute's counterterrorism center, adds: "I think the knee-jerk response will be to blame the messenger. But the jihadists are already using the Internet. The real issue is how we counter these messages of hate and radicalism."[90]

CHAPTER 6

THE FUTURE OF ONLINE SOCIAL NETWORKING

Online social networking is more than just a fad. Every day, it evolves and adapts to users. Some people welcome this change, while others fear it. What started out as a place for friends to hang out online is being embraced by people of all ages and backgrounds. Businesses, politicians, churches, libraries, and activists all experience the power of these sites. Social networks are not just for spare-time fun anymore. They are swiftly becoming an integral part of daily life. New users, new uses, and even new forms of online social networking are all changes that will create the future of social networking.

A Business World

Shari Chiara, a marketing manager at IBM Corporation, logs on to the company's networking site, Beehive, to check on what her coworkers are doing. Since Chiara works from home in New York, she often felt isolated from coworkers around the world. Now with Beehive, "I'm more in touch with people worldwide," she says. "I'll go on and there'll be comments from people in Japan, Australia."[91]

Since the introduction of Beehive at IBM in 2007, more than twenty-nine thousand employees have joined the networking site. The internal site is similar to traditional social networking sites like MySpace and Facebook. It allows users to post photos and other information. Sites can be open to the entire company or restricted to connections. "You connect with people that are further away on a more personal level,"[92] said Chiara.

Companies like IBM, Procter and Gamble, and Nortel Networks Corporation have taken notice of the popularity of social networking and recognized a tool they can put to good use. In recent years more employees work from home or are scattered geographically. In addition, business is more global. Customers, vendors, and consultants may work in different countries and time zones. The technology of social networking is a way to pull these groups together in a common forum. "When you have people geographically dispersed, you need to provide an interactive and immersive and intimate environment that allows them to feel communication is very natural,"[93] said Kelly Kanellakis at Nortel Networks Corporation.

BUSINESSES DEVELOPING SOCIAL NETWORKS FOR EMPLOYEES

"This is very much in its infancy. . . . It's right now in the hands of people who 'get it,' but in the next several years that could tip and it could become core to how people work together." —Joe Schueller, global business service innovation manager at Procter and Gamble.

Quoted in Barbara Rose, "Social Networks Link Workers," *Chicago Tribune*, June 17, 2008. www.chicagotribune.com/business/chi-tue-corporate-social networkjun17,0, 1112300.story.

Some employers bet that social networks will allow employees to become more productive and work together better. "We believe innovation will happen a lot more quickly," said Kanellakis. "And because we've got such a web of communications, it'll spread a lot more quickly."[94]

The growth of LinkedIn demonstrates the interest of business professionals in social networking. LinkedIn is a social network that targets career-focused, white-collar workers. LinkedIn users are generally looking to network with other professionals instead of searching for the next party. The users of LinkedIn are older, with an average age of forty-one. Users can post online résumés and search for experts to help solve business problems. Users link to other coworkers and business contacts. Through this

Many companies have created internal networking sites as a way of connecting employees, some of whom may work at home or in disparate offices, as well as customers and vendors.

network, they can get introductions to more business contacts. "We want to create a broad and critical business tool that is used by tens of millions of business professionals every day to make them better at what they do,"[95] said Dan Nye, chief executive at LinkedIn.

A new feature on LinkedIn, Company Groups, lets all the employees from a company on the site gather together in a private Web forum. "This is a collected, protected space for employees to talk to each other and reference outside information,"[96] said Reid Hoffman, founder and chair of LinkedIn. LinkedIn believes that more companies will sign on to their site as they recognize the benefits of employees working together online. According to Jeffrey Glass, a partner at Bain Capital and an investor in LinkedIn, "This is a powerful tool because inside the corporation, there are massive bodies of knowledge and relationships between individuals that the corporation has been unable to take advantage of until now."[97]

Marketing on Networks

Social networking is also changing how businesses market their products. Text alerts, sending updates on Twitter, and creating a blog are all ways to market online. Other businesses may set up a profile page on Facebook or MySpace that features pictures, reviews, and links to outside Web sites.

Zane Hagy owns a public relations business that uses online social networking as a core piece of his clients' marketing plans. He works on blogs for eight clients and also sends out updates on Twitter. "There's a built-in audience, and companies are trying to figure out ways to leverage that to their advantage," he said. "There are so many different ways to put themselves in front of potential clients. It's fascinating."[98]

Suzy Trotta, a real estate agent, started a real estate blog in February 2008. She also sends out Twitter updates. At first she did not notice any substantial increase in clients. After a few months, however, she saw the momentum. "It takes awhile, but I've made connections," said Trotta. "There are those who are not ready to buy or sell yet but say they will call me because they feel like they know me and trust me."[99]

Want to Be a Twitterer?

What are you doing? That is the Twitter question. A free social networking and microblogging service, Twitter users send the answer to their network of followers. In 140 characters or less, the message is a "tweet." Users can get tweets on the Internet, desktop applications like Twhirl, or mobile devices. People choose to follow users based on the "tweets" sent. The more interesting the tweets, the more followers a user will have.

Some business professionals and entrepreneurs are twittering away. They have found it can be a good resource for connecting with industry professionals, keeping up-to-date on trends, and sharing ideas. "Where Twitter is cool is that you're able to see what people are work-

ing on. It's a tool to bring more people into your life, whether personally or professionally, and to get your voice heard," explained Al Krueger, founder of a strategic branding and public relations firm.

Experienced Twitterers warn newbies to put some fun into their tweets. "If you're all business on Twitter, it doesn't work," said Kelly Fitzsimmons, CEO of an online joke-telling service. "If you put more of yourself into it, and you're sharing your world, what you're doing, what you're seeing, people respond well to that."

Quoted in Tannette Johnson-Elie, "Twitter Blends Online Networking, Instant Messaging," *Milwaukee Journal Sentinel*, June 24, 2008. www.jsonline.com/story/index.aspx?id=765641.

Getting Out the Vote

The 2008 U.S. presidential primaries and election ushered social networking into the political spotlight. According to a Pew Internet & American Life Project study, 46 percent of Americans used the Internet to get news about the campaign or share their opinions on the candidates. This was a significant increase from the 31 percent who used the Internet at the same point in the 2004 election. The Pew study also found that 35 percent of Americans had watched campaign videos online. In addition 40 percent of Americans with social network profiles or 10 percent of all Americans used social networking sites for political reasons. Young adults drove this surge in online political activity. The study found that half of all young adults with social network profiles used these sites to research candidates or volunteer for a campaign.

The 2008 presidential election saw candidates turn to online social networking in order to promote their platforms, keep voters informed of campaign details, mobilize supporters, and collect donations.

Illinois senator Barack Obama used Web and social networking tools to connect with voters during his presidential campaign. His team designed a site that was similar to Facebook. On MyBarackObama.com, supporters could join local groups, organize events, and read the campaign's blog.

People also used the site to donate to Obama's campaign, raising millions of dollars from everyday Americans. Obama himself saw social networking as key to his campaign. "One of my fundamental beliefs from my days as a community organizer is that real change comes from the bottom up," he said in a statement. "And there's no more powerful tool for grass-roots organizing than the Internet."[100]

Another 2008 presidential candidate, Ron Paul, was relatively unknown prior to his campaign. Through the efforts of grassroots supporters online, the Paul campaign raised a record $4 million dollars in a single day. A few weeks later the campaign broke its own record and raised over $6 million in a twenty-four-hour period. Paul supporters were active on blogs, online polls, and social networks. While other candidates had more money and the support of the major political parties, Paul proved that an active online community can launch a lesser-known candidate into the spotlight. The low-cost Internet may become a way for future political candidates to bring their message to the public without the financial backing of the major political parties.

The success of Obama's and Paul's social networking strategies sparked interest from other political candidates. "Their use of social networks will guide the way for future campaigns,"[101] said Peter Daou, Internet director for presidential primary candidate Hillary Clinton. Candidates have realized the importance of social networking to their campaigns. According to Alan Rosenblatt, a blogger at TechPresident, the example set by the 2008 campaign sends a clear message. "Not only do voters use the Internet to learn about the candidates and the issues, but they are sharing it with others," he said. "This is most important. It means that what people learn on the Internet influences nearly everyone in the country."[102]

Say a Little Prayer

Social networks are also expanding into churches. Christian leaders recognize that social networks allow them to keep in touch more effectively with youth ministry, college groups, and other church groups. Dale Tadlock is the associate pastor of a Baptist church. He uses Facebook to keep in touch with the young people at his church and send out event reminders. "It has given me a great opportunity to work with students," he says. "It's become a way to stay informed."[103]

On Churches Using Social Networks

"I think it's just changed the way we are interacting and the way we are doing things. I think it literally has changed our culture." —Dane Tadlock, assistant pastor of the First Baptist Church of Waynesboro, Virginia.

Quoted in Rachel Mehlhaff, "Jesus in MySpace: Churches Use Social Networking Sites," *Associated Baptist Press*, July 3, 2008. www.abpnews.com/index.php?option=com_content&task=view&id=3392&Itemid=53.

Other churches choose to join MyChurch.org, a social networking site built for congregations. MyChurch users can send messages to specific users or to groups. They announce prayer requests and advertise events. They also use the site to share photos, audio files, and comment on sermons.

Each church has a moderator who reviews its site's content to ensure that it follows the church's guidelines. The moderator may also review individual member sites. MyChurch even has an application that allows users to put their MyChurch content onto their Facebook page. This connection allows the users' Facebook friends to know what is going on at their church.

Online Activists

In past generations, people who were passionate about a cause relied on word of mouth, paper flyers, and face-to-face club meetings to spread the news about their activities. Today more people turn to the Internet for information about volunteering and social causes. Online, organizations for social causes can set up profiles and quickly gather thousands of followers. There are even social networks such as YouthNoise.com that specifically target young people who are interested in working for social change.

Individual activists can decorate their Web pages with photos of volunteer events and write blogs about their efforts. They can send e-mails from home computers in support of a cause to politicians, corporate executives, or newspaper editors.

Getting the word out about the latest event or rally is as easy as sending an e-mail, text alert, or profile update. In 2006 over one hundred thousand students in a California public school district skipped class on May 1 in support of immigration rights. Many of the students learned about the protest and the immigration issue through comments and pages on MySpace.com.

Books Can Be Friends

Other groups such as libraries and authors use social networking to advertise programs and book launches. Libraries with profiles on Facebook and MySpace communicate with users on the latest news and programs through profile entries. MySpace blogs allow authors to update readers with the latest information on appearances, reading, or television interviews.

Many authors see social networks as a way to increase buzz about their books. Author Brad Listi blogs every day on his MySpace page to promote his novel. He believes that the site helps his readers get to know him in a more personal way. "What I do doesn't involve any kind of hard sell," he said. "It involved taking the time to write each day, answering all correspondences with readers, and building a fan base in a personal, organic, and entertaining way."[104]

Author Marcy Dermansky used her MySpace page and Top 8 Friends list to promote her novel. All eight of her "friends" have the same names as the characters in her book. She searched the site for people with the needed names, including some unusual ones like Yumiko and Smita, and approached them with her idea. Some were so receptive they ended up buying her book to learn more about their character.

Dermansky believes that using MySpace to promote her book helped increase sales and improve her name recognition as an author. She also believes that the site helps her to be more accessible to readers. "It's intimidating to write a fan letter to an author. There is the fear of being dorky or inarticulate. But in the MySpace universe, somehow that kind of inhibition and difficulty has been broken down,"[105] she said.

New Forms of Social Networking

Besides the ever-expanding groups of new users online, the way in which people experience social networks will also evolve. The initial thrill of MySpace and Facebook may give way to more specific niche sites as users target their interests. Many new sites cater to smaller, more focused groups of people.

One example of a niche site that aims to connect athletes with recruiters and coaches is beRecruited.com. Alison Wong, a seventeen-year-old hockey player, signed on to the site after her father

Sports Teams Attract Fans Online

The Washington Glory, a fast-pitch softball team, demonstrates how lesser-known sporting teams can use social networks to build a fan base. The team signed up for a MySpace page last year. Owner Paul Wilson uses the site to send out coupons for discounted admissions to games and respond to messages from fans. Whenever he sees a young girl thanking a player for answering her online message, he knows the site is working. "Now they communicate so much through online or text messages," said Wilson. "So instead of getting them to come to us, I wanted to go to them."

Because social network advertising is free, teams in the less popular profes-sional leagues can afford the online promotion. Lacking national exposure, these teams frequently target a niche market. Online media provides the perfect opportunity to reach potential fans successfully.

Teams from more popular professional sports have taken notice. Major League Baseball planned to set up a Facebook profile in late 2008. Teams from the NFL, NBA, and NHL have already started using social networks to reach fans.

Quoted in Mark Viera, "Befriending Generation Facebook," *Washington Post*, July 15, 2008. www.washingtonpost.com/wp-dyn/content/article/2008/07/14/AR2008071402144.html.

discovered it online. She posted information that colleges might be interested in—SAT scores, hockey stats, and some personal information. She also included the link to her beRecruited profile on her college applications. Within a few months, she had offers from several schools that wanted her to play hockey for them. She said:

> It definitely opened doors to schools that I might never have thought about playing for. It's a great way to connect with coaches and get your name out there, and it was cheaper than long-distance phone calls or driving down to talk to coaches, so I'm pretty sure my parents were happy about that.[106]

Other services, like Ning, allow users to create their own social networks. Users can customize the network to focus on their own specific interests, companies, fans, and friends. Artists, athletes, journalists, students, parents, crafters, and special interest groups all have created social networks through Ning. Marc Andreessen, cofounder of Ning, believes in the appeal of custom networks. "The existing social networks are fantastic but they put users in a straitjacket . . . they were not built to be flexible," he says. "They do not let people build and design their own worlds, which is the nature of what people want to do online."[107]

As more social networks spring up, it will be inconvenient for users to enter the same information into multiple sites. A megasite or another way to transfer information between sites appears to be inevitable. Marc Canter supports OpenID, a project that would let users easily transfer profile information among several social networks. "Humans are migratory beasts, and we do not want to re-enter our data every time we join a new site," he said. "Users own their data and should be able to move it around freely."[108]

Mobile Social Networks

Many people predict that one of the next steps for social networks is going mobile. "Kids want to be connected to their friends at all times," said Howard Hartenbaum, a partner at a venture capital firm. "They can't do that when you turn off the

Mobile technology is expected to drive the future of online social networking,
allowing users access via their cell phones and other portable electronic devices.

computer."[109] Powerful mobile gadgets and online services will help users send out mobile messages about the latest details in their lives.

CAN THERE BE TOO MUCH COMMUNICATION?

"Getting all kinds of communication in such a remote place is a bit confusing. I kept responding, 'I don't really have the time to talk to you now. I have to make photos of these elephants.'" —Walter Zai, answering mobile social network messages while on safari in South Africa.

Quoted in Brad Stone and Matt Richtel, "Social Networking Leaves Confines of the Computer," *New York Times*, April 30, 2007. www.nytimes.com/2007/04/30/technology/30social.html.

Walter Zai, an engineer, kept a digital diary while on safari in South Africa. He used an online service called Kyte to send out updates and pictures to his network from his mobile phone. "You feel like you are instantly broadcasting your own life and experience to your friends at home, and to anyone in the world who wants to join,"[110] said Zai.

Changing How People Interact

As more people embrace social networks, the line between the real world and the online world will start to fade. In many cases, social networks and online activity has already impacted how people interact with each other and behave away from their computers.

Professionally, social networks foster collaboration among spread-out groups. Before, it was difficult and expensive to share information and ideas with people in different geographic locations. Using social networks, scientists share details on research projects and get input from colleagues around the world. Teachers gather to share ideas and projects for the classroom. Even businesspeople can turn online for solutions to common company problems with vendors, customers, and employees.

Social networks also impact the way in which people interact with each other on a personal level. Before social networks, people engaged in hours of small talk to learn each other's favorite foods, movies, and pet peeves. Over time, they revealed details about their own life, family, and emotions.

Now users can search online for people they have just met. Suddenly, there is no need for hours of small talk. Users can learn all about a new friend just by reading their social network profile. Some of this research occurs even before people meet in person. By researching online, many people discover the personal details about a casual acquaintance that used to be reserved knowledge for close friends.

Changing How People Mourn

Many young people have found that social networks give them a comfortable place to express their feelings about the passing of a friend or family member. When Deborah Lee Walker, a twenty-three-year-old, died in an automobile accident, her father logged on to her MySpace page and found many messages from friends expressing sorrow over her death.

Reading messages and visiting the page of a deceased friend or loved one can provide comfort. "I still believe that even though she's not the one on her MySpace page, that's a way I can reach out to her," said Jenna Finke about a friend who died recently. "Her really close friends go on there every day. It means a lot to know people aren't forgetting her."[111]

Others are disturbed by the public nature of what has traditionally been a private matter. Some families can become overwhelmed by messages from strangers. In some cases they reach out to the families for help in dealing with their own loss. To Walker's mother, these messages were not welcome. "The grief of our own friends and family is almost more than we can bear on top of our own, and we don't need anyone else's on our shoulders."[112]

Creating a Global Community

Before social networking, many people primarily interacted with others in the same community and nearby regions. Often, phone calls and travel to far away places were too expensive to keep up regular contact. For many people, letters to a pen pal were the only contact they had with a person from another country.

Online social networks allow users to connect with others on the next block or on the other side of the world.

Now, with the widespread availability of computers and the Internet, everyday citizens are able to connect with people across the world on a regular basis. It is as easy to talk online with a friend in India as one who lives across the street. Users might initially find each other through a shared interest in a specific hobby. That initial contact may gradually lead to more conversations and understanding about different cultures, languages, and experiences. In this way some people believe that social networking will bring people together in a global community. The technology will break down geographical and political barriers.

How will online social networking change in the future? The impact that past innovations like the printing press, radio, and television would have was not completely clear at their introduction. As more people move online, social networking may become a natural extension of human interaction, like the telephone and e-mail. Eston Bond, a Web designer, believes that "social media will do more than affect the teenagers and twenty-somethings. Social media will be the core of the common human cause. . . . I can't tell you exactly what the future of social networks will be; I can just tell you what we are capable of making them to be."[113]

Introduction: The Explosion of Online Social Networking

1. Quoted in Carol Brydolf, "Minding MySpace: Balancing the Benefits and Risks of Students' Online Social Networks," *Education Digest*, October 2007. www.csba.org/NewsAndMedia/Publications/CASchoolsMagazine/2007/ Spring/InThisIssue/Minding_MySpace.aspx.

2. Quoted in Anthony Williams, "Putting Life Online Could Haunt Later," *Houston Chronicle*, June 29, 2008.

3. Quoted in Brydolf, "Minding MySpace."

Chapter 1: What Is Online Social Networking?

4. Quoted in Patricia Sellers, "MySpace Cowboys," *Fortune*, September 4, 2006. http://money.cnn.com/magazines/fortune/fortune_archive/2006/09/04/8384727/index.htm.

5. Quoted in Sellers, "MySpace Cowboys."

6. Quoted in Alex Wright, "Friending, Ancient or Otherwise," *New York Times*, December 2, 2007. www.nytimes.com/2007/12/02/weekinreview/02wright.html.

7. Quoted in Wright, "Friending, Ancient or Otherwise."

8. Quoted in Wright, "Friending, Ancient or Otherwise."

9. Quoted in Wright, "Friending, Ancient or Otherwise."

Chapter 2: Teens and Online Social Networking

10. Quoted in Anastasia Goodstein, *Totally Wired: What Teens and Tweens Are Really Doing Online*. New York: St. Martin's, 2007, p. 53.

11. Quoted in Larry Magid and Anne Collier, *MySpace Unraveled: A Parent's Guide to Teen Social Networking*. Berkeley, CA: Peachpit, 2007, p. 16.

12. Quoted in Connie Neal, *MySpace for Moms and Dads*. Grand Rapids, MI: Zondervan, 2007, p. 29.

13. Quoted in Goodstein, *Totally Wired*, p. 22.

14. Quoted in Goodstein, *Totally Wired*, p. 34.

15. Goodstein, *Totally Wired*, p. 66.

16. Quoted in Candice M. Kelsey, *Generation MySpace: Helping Your Teen Survive Online Adolescence*. New York: Marlowe, 2007, p. 14.

17. Quoted in Hattie Kauffman, "Social Networking: An Internet Addiction," CBS News.com, June 24, 2008. www.cbs news.com/stories/2008/06/24/earlyshow/main4205009 .shtml?source=search_story.

18. Quoted in Kelsey, *Generation MySpace*, p. 14.

19. Quoted in Kauffman, "Social Networking."

20. Quoted in Kelsey, *Generation MySpace*, p. 149.

21. Quoted in Kelsey, *Generation MySpace*, p. 157.

22. Quoted in Robin M. Lowalski, Susan P. Limber, and Patricia W. Agatston, *Cyber Bullying*. Maldon, MA: Blackwell, 2008, p. 42.

23. Quoted in Kelsey, *Generation MySpace*, p. 111.

24. Quoted in Kelsey, *Generation MySpace*, p. 120.

25. Magid and Collier, *MySpace Unraveled*, p. 12.

Chapter 3: Who Is Responsible for Social Network Safety?

26. Quoted in Rob Stafford, "Why Parents Must Mind MySpace," MSNBC.com, April 5, 2006. www.msnbc.msn.com/ed/11064451.

27. Quoted in Stafford, "Why Parents Must Mind MySpace."

28. Quoted in Cindy Long, "I Need My Space!" *NEA Today*, April 2007. www.nea.org/home/11405.htm.

29. Quoted in Julie Steenhuysen, "Study Rejects Internet Sex Predator Stereotype," Reuters.com, February 18, 2008. www .reuters.com/article/internetNews/idUSN1560642020 80218?pageNumber=2&virtualBrandChannel=0.

30. Quoted in Steenhuysen, "Study Rejects Internet Sex Predator Stereotype."

31. Quoted in Steenhuysen, "Study Rejects Internet Sex Predator Stereotype."

32. Quoted in Kelsey, *Generation MySpace*, p. 173.

33. Quoted in Kelsey, *Generation MySpace*, p. 174.

34. Quoted in Kelsey, *Generation MySpace*, p. 177.

35. Quoted in Kelsey, *Generation MySpace*, p. 181.

36. Quoted in Tom Tapp, "Porn Star Promotion Predicament Leads to MySpace Advertiser Revolt," *Hollywood Wiretap*, May 24, 2006. www.hollywoodwiretap.com/?module=news&action=story&id=2315.

37. MySpace.com, "MySpace.com Terms of Use Agreement." www.myspace.com/index.cfm?fuseaction=misc.terms.

38. Quoted in ABCNews, "What Are Teens Hiding on MySpace," May 18, 2006. http://abcnews.go.com/print?id=197 5086.

39. Quoted in Kate Fillion, "Problems Happen in Any Community. The Sense MySpace Is Where All These Bad Things Are Happening Is Overblown," *Maclean's*, May 14, 2007. www.macleans.ca/article.jsp?content=20070514_105154_105154.

40. Danah Boyd and Henry Jenkins, "MySpace and Deleting Online Predators Act (DOPA)," *MIT Tech Talk*, May 26, 2006. www.danah.org/papers/MySpaceDOPA.html.

41. Quoted in Tara Bahrampour and Lori Aratani, "Teens' Bold Blogs Alarm Area Schools," *Washington Post*, January 17, 2006. www.washingtonpost.com/wp-dyn/content/article/20 06/01/16/AR2006011601489_2.html.

42. Boyd and Jenkins, "MySpace and Deleting Online Predators Act (DOPA)."

43. Quoted in Goodstein, *Totally Wired*, p. 104.

44. Quoted in Bob Sullivan, "Kids, Blogs and Too Much Information," MSNBC.com, April 29, 2005. www.msnbc.msn.com/id/7668788.

Chapter 4: The Blurred Line Between Private and Public Lives

45. Quoted in Tara Bahrampour, "On the Web, 'Dear Diary' Becomes 'Dear World,'" *Washington Post*, January 7, 2007. www.washingtonpost.com/wp-dyn/content/article/2007/01/01/AR2007010100758.html.

46. Quoted in Bahrampour, "On the Web, 'Dear Diary' Becomes 'Dear World.'"

47. Quoted in Bahrampour, "On the Web, 'Dear Diary' Becomes 'Dear World.'"

48. Quoted in Bahrampour, "On the Web, 'Dear Diary' Becomes 'Dear World.'"

49. Quoted in Amanda Lenhart and Mary Madden, *Teens, Privacy & Online Social Networks*. Pew Internet & American Life Project, April 18, 2007, p. 28. www.pewinternet.org/pdfs/PIP_Teens_Privacy_SNS_Report_Final.pdf.

50. Quoted in Lenhart and Madden, *Teens, Privacy & Online Social Networks*, p. 24.

51. Quoted in Lenhart and Madden, *Teens, Privacy & Online Social Networks*, p. 25.

52. Quoted in Martha Irvine, "Privacy Becomes Concern as Social Online Sites Become Fair Game," *USA Today*, December 30, 2006. www.usatoday.com/tech/news/2006-12-30privacy-online_x.htm.

53. Quoted in Martha Irvine, "Online Privacy More Complicated than It Seems," Courant.com, June 22, 2008. www.courant.com/features/lifestyle/hc-privacy.artjun22,0,1782562.story.

54. Quoted in Kim Hart, "A Flashy Facebook Page, at a Cost to Privacy," *Washington Post*, June 12, 2008. www.washingtonpost.com/wpdyn/content/article/2008/06/11/AR2008061103759.html.

55. Quoted in Irvine, "Online Privacy More Complicated than It Seems."

56. Quoted in Goodstein, *Totally Wired*, p. 36.

57. Quoted in Sullivan, "Kids, Blogs and Too Much Information."

58. Quoted in Lenhart and Madden, *Teens, Privacy & Online Social Networks*, p. 15.

59. Quoted in Lenhart and Madden, *Teens, Privacy & Online Social Networks*, p. 19.

60. Quoted in Bahrampour and Aratani, "Teens' Bold Blogs Alarm Area Schools."

61. Quoted in Bahrampour and Aratani, "Teens' Bold Blogs Alarm Area Schools."

62. Quoted in Janet Kornblum and Mary Beth Marklein, "What You Say Online Could Haunt You," *USA Today*, March 8, 2006. www.usatoday.com/tech/news/internetprivacy/2006-03-08-facebook-myspace_x.htm.

63. Quoted in Kornblum and Marklein, "What You Say Online Could Haunt You."

64. Quoted in Alan Finder, "For Some, Online Persona Undermines a Resume," *New York Times*, June 11, 2006. www.nytimes.com/2006/06/11/us/11recruit.html.

65. Quoted in Finder, "For Some, Online Persona Undermines a Resume."

66. Quoted in Finder, "For Some, Online Persona Undermines a Resume."

67. Quoted in Finder, "For Some, Online Persona Undermines a Resume."

68. Quoted in Finder, "For Some, Online Persona Undermines a Resume."

69. Quoted in Janet Kornblum, "Social, Work Lives Collide on Networking Websites," *USA Today*, January 18, 2008. www.usatoday.com/tech/webguide/internetlife/2008-01-17-social-network-nobarriers_N.htm.

70. Quoted in Irvine, "Privacy Becomes Concern as Social Online Sites Become Fair Game."

71. Quoted in Williams, "Putting Life Online Could Haunt Later."

72. Quoted in Williams, "Putting Life Online Could Haunt Later."

73. Quoted in Ari Melber, "About Facebook," *Nation*, January 7–14, 2008. www.thenation.com/doc/20080107/melber.

Chapter 5: The Threat of Cyberterrorism

74. National Conference of State Legislatures, "Cyberterrorism." www.ncsl.org/programs/lis/cip/cyberterrorism.htm.

75. Quoted in John Wildermuth, "Cyber-Threat Rising, Chertoff Says. Homeland Security Boss Speaks to Group in Silicon Valley," *San Francisco Chronicle*, July 29, 2005.

76. Quoted in *PC Magazine Online*, "Security Experts Split on 'Cyberterrorism' Threat," April 16, 2008.

77. Quoted in Robert Lenzner and Nathan Vardi, "Cyber-nightmare," *Forbes Global*, September 20, 2004. www.forbes .com/global/2004/0920/104.html.

78. Quoted in Lenzner and Vardi, "Cyber nightmare."

79. Quoted in *InformationWeek*, "'Electronic Jihad' App Offers Cyber Terrorism for the Masses; U.S. Businesses Would Be Greatly Impacted by Any Large-Scale Cyberattacks Because Most of That Infrastructure Is Run by Companies in the Private Sector," July 2, 2007. www.informationweek.com/news/ internet/showArticle.jhtml?articleID=200001943.

80. Quoted in *InformationWeek*, "'Electronic Jihad' App Offers Cyber Terrorism for the Masses."

81. Quoted in Kasie Hunt, "Osama bin Laden Fan Clubs Build Online Communities," *USA Today*, March 8, 2006. www.usa today.com/tech/news/2006-03-08-orkut-al-qaeda_x.htm.

82. Quoted in Hunt, "Osama bin Laden Fan Clubs Build Online Communities."

83. Quoted in Rita Katz and Josh Devon, "Web of Terror," *Forbes Global*, May 7, 2007. http://members.forbes.com/forbes/ 2007/0507/184a.html.

84. Quoted in Graham Rayman and John Moreno Gonzales, "Chat Rooms Can Net Cyber Terrorists," *Newsday*, July 8, 2006.

85. Quoted in Rayman and Gonzales, "Chat Rooms Can Net Cyber Terrorists."

86. Quoted in *The Science Show*, "How Terrorists Use the Internet," ABC Radio National, March 31, 2007. www.abc .net.au/rn/scienceshow/stories/2007/1885902.htm#tran script.

87. Quoted in Isabelle Groc, "The Online Hunt for Terrorists," PCmag.com, February 27, 2008. www.pcmag.com/article2/0, 2704,2270962,00.asp.

88. Quoted in Groc, "The Online Hunt for Terrorists."

89. Quoted in Hunt, "Osama bin Laden Fan Clubs Build Online Communities."

90. Quoted in Hunt, "Osama bin Laden Fan Clubs Build Online Communities."

Chapter 6: The Future of Online Social Networking

91. Quoted in Barbara Rose, "Social Networks Link Workers," *Chicago Tribune*, June 17, 2008. www.chicagotribune.com/business/chi-tue-corporate-social-networkjun17,0,1112300.story.

92. Quoted in Rose, "Social Networks Link Workers."

93. Quoted in Rose, "Social Networks Link Workers."

94. Quoted in Rose, "Social Networks Link Workers."

95. Quoted in Brad Stone, "At Social Site, Only the Businesslike Need Apply," *New York Times*, June 18, 2008. www.nytimes.com/2008/06/18/technology/18linkedin.html?_r=1&scp=1&sq=At%20Social%20Site,%20Only%20the%20Businesslike%20Need%20Apply&st=cse.

96. Quoted in Stone, "At Social Site, Only the Businesslike Need Apply."

97. Quoted in Stone, "At Social Site, Only the Businesslike Need Apply."

98. Quoted in Carly Harrington, "All a Twitter: Businesses Keyed Up About Using Social Networking to Create Relationships with Customers," *Knoxville News Sentinel*, June 15, 2008. www.knoxnews.com/news/2008/Jun/15/all-a-twitter/.

99. Quoted in Harrington, "All a Twitter."

100. Quoted in Brian Stelter, "Obama Harnesses Power of Web Social Networking," *Seattle Times*, July 7, 2008. http://seattletimes.nwsource.com/html/politics/2008036639_obamaface07.html.

101. Quoted in Stelter, "Obama Harnesses Power of Web Social Networking."

102. Quoted in Heather Havenstein, "Web Use in 2008 Political Campaigns Shattering Records in U.S.," *Computerworld*, June 18, 2008. www.computerworld.com/action/article.do?command=viewArticleBasic&articleId=9100038.

103. Quoted in Rachel Mehlhaff, "Jesus in MySpace: Churches Use Social-Networking Sites," *Associated Baptist Press*, July 3, 2008. www.abpnews.com/index.php?option=com_content&task=view&id=3392&Itemid=53.

104. Quoted in Rachel Kramer Bussel, "How Many Friends Does

Your Book Have?" Mediabistro.com, August 7, 2006 www .mediabistro.com/articles/cache/a8194.asp.

105. Quoted in Bussel, "How Many Friends Does Your Book Have?"

106. Quoted in Matt Hartley, "She Shoots, She Scores with On-line Recruiters," *Globe and Mail*, June 27, 2008. www.the globeandmail.com/servlet/story/RTGAM.20080627.wl teampages27/BNStory/PersonalTech/home.

107. Quoted in Brad Stone, "Social Networking's Next Phase," *New York Times*, March 3, 2007. www.nytimes.com/2007/ 03/03/technology/03social.html.

108. Quoted in Stone, "Social Networking's Next Phase."

109. Quoted in Brad Stone and Matt Richtel, "Social Network-ing Leaves Confines of the Computer," *New York Times*, April 30, 2007. www.nytimes.com/2007/04/30/technology/ 30social.html.

110. Quoted in Stone and Richtel, "Social Networking Leaves Confines of the Computer."

111. Quoted in Warren St. John, "Rituals of Grief Go Online," *New York Times*, April 27, 2006. www.nytimes.com/2006/ 04/27/technology/27myspace.html.

112. Quoted in St. John, "Rituals of Grief Go Online."

113. Eston Bond, "Eston Bond on the Future of Social Network-ing," O'ReillydiyIncite MySpace blog, October 10, 2006. http://blog.myspace.com/index.cfm?fuseaction=blog.view& friendID=101972072&blogID=179258294.

Chapter 1: What Is Online Social Networking?

1. What factors influenced the rise of online social networking?

2. According to the author, why did MySpace achieve success when earlier social networking sites did not?

3. What are the differences between open and closed social networks? According to the author, what are the advantages and disadvantages of each?

Chapter 2: Teens and Online Social Networking

1. How does social networking fulfill adolescent developmental needs?

2. According to the author, how do social networks influence and contribute to teens' negative behavior?

3. Why does cyberbullying impact victims in a more personal and relentless way than traditional bullying?

Chapter 3: Who Is Responsible for Social Network Safety?

1. Is banning social networking sites entirely an appropriate and effective way to keep users safe?

2. What measures should users take to ensure personal safety?

3. With the adult world dangers online, should social networks be segregated between teen and adult users?

Chapter 4: The Blurred Line Between Private and Public Lives

1. How has the meaning of personal privacy changed since the introduction of social networks?

2. How do users decide what information to post online? What are the risks of sharing personal information?

3. As more people move online, what conflicts may arise between personal and public lives?

Chapter 5: The Threat of Cyberterrorism

1. In what ways has social networking enabled terrorists? How has it hindered them?

2. In what ways is the United States vulnerable to terrorist attack? How have the Internet and social networking helped to expose these weaknesses?

3. Should known terrorist Web sites be shut down? Or are they valuable sources of information for law enforcement?

Chapter 6: The Future of Online Social Networking

1. How is social networking expanding beyond purely social uses?

2. In what ways does social networking change human behavior? Are these changes desirable?

3. How is social networking bringing the world closer together?

ORGANIZATIONS TO CONTACT

American Civil Liberties Union (ACLU)
Web site: www.aclu.org

The ACLU is a nonprofit organization that believes civil liberties must be respected, even in times of national emergency. The ACLU has been active in several cases involving free-speech rights and on-line social networking. The ACLU has an affiliate in every state and Puerto Rico, which can be contacted through the ACLU Web site.

Center for Safe and Responsible Internet Use
474 W. 29th Ave.
Eugene, OR 97405
phone: (541) 556-1145
e-mail: info@csriu.org
Web site: http://new.csriu.org

The Center for Safe and Responsible Internet Use provides research and outreach services to address issues of the safe and responsible use of the Internet. The site offers student guides to cyberbullying and cyber threats.

ConnectSafely
706 Colorado Ave.
Palo Alto, CA 94303
Web site: www.connectsafely.org

ConnectSafely is for parents, teens, educators, and advocates interested in the impact of the social Web. The site has tips for teens and parents and resources for safe blogging and social networking.

i-SAFE
5900 Pasteur Ct., Ste. 100
Carlsbad, CA 92008

phone: (760) 603-7911
fax: (760) 603-8382
Web site: www.i-safe.org

This nonprofit foundation's mission is to educate and empower youth to make their Internet experiences safe and responsible. The goal is to educate students on how to avoid dangerous, inappropriate, or unlawful online behavior.

Web Wise Kids
PO Box 28203
Santa Ana, CA 92799
phone: (866) 932-9473
fax: (714) 435-0523
e-mail: info@webwisekids.org
Web site: www.webwisekids.org

Web Wise Kids is a unique organization that offers fun, challenging, and interactive programs for classroom and home use that show kids about predators who use the Internet.

WiredSafety
e-mail: webmaster@wiredsafety.org
Web site: www.wiredsafety.org

WiredSafety provides help, information, and education to Internet and mobile device users of all ages. Its Web site helps with issues of online fraud, cyber stalking, child safety, and cyberbullying.

Books

Sylvia Engdahl, *Online Social Networking*. Farmington Hills, MI: Greenhaven, 2007. A young adult title that presents arguments on the positive and negative aspects of online social networking.

Anastasia Goodstein, *Totally Wired: What Teens and Tweens Are Really Doing Online*. New York: St. Martin's, 2007. An inside guide to what teens are doing online and how they are using technology.

Candice M. Kelsey, *Generation MySpace: Helping Your Teen Survive Online Adolescence*. New York: Marlowe, 2007. Features interviews with hundreds of teens about the benefits and pitfalls of MySpace and social networking.

Barbara A. Lewis, *The Teen Guide to Global Action: How to Connect with Others (Near & Far) to Create Social Change*. Minneapolis, MN: Free Spirit, 2008. Features hands-on ideas for teens to get involved online in volunteerism and social activism.

Larry Magid and Anne Collier, *MySpace Unraveled: A Parent's Guide to Teen Social Networking*. Berkeley, CA: Peachpit, 2007. Discusses the basics of using MySpace and creating a safe online experience.

Connie Neal, *MySpace for Moms and Dads*. Grand Rapids, MI: Zondervan, 2007. A quick overview of MySpace, what it is, how it works, and why it is important to teens.

Nancy Willard, *Cyber-Safe Kids, Cyber-Savvy Teens: Helping Young People Learn to Use the Internet Safely and Responsibly*. San Francisco: Wiley, 2007. Gives strategies for kids and teens to use the Internet safely and responsibly.

Periodicals

Tara Bahrampour, "On the Web, 'Dear Diary' Becomes 'Dear World,'" *Washington Post*, January 7, 2007.

Tara Bahrampour and Lori Aratani, "Teens' Bold Blogs Alarm Area Schools," *Washington Post*, January 17, 2006.

Internet Sources

Pew Internet & American Life Project, *Social Networking Websites and Teens: An Overview*. January 3, 2007. www.pewinternet .org/pdfs/PIP_SNS_Data_Memo_Jan_2007.pdf.

Pew Internet & American Life Project, *Teens and Social Media*. December 19, 2007. www.pewinternet.org/pdfs/PIP_Teens_ Social_Media_Final.pdf.

Pew Internet & American Life Project, *Teens, Privacy & Online Social Networks*. April 18, 2007. www.pewinternet.org/pdfs/PIP_ Teens_Privacy_SNS_Report_Final.pdf.

Web Sites

National Conference for State Legislatures, Cyberterrorism (www.ncsl.org/programs/lis/cip/cyberterrorism.htm). This site provides access to legislation, statutes, and government resources on cyberterrorism.

Wired Kids (www.wiredkids.org/wiredkids_org.html). Wired Kids is a Web site that helps kids learn about online issues and educates about how to use the Internet in a positive way.

WiredSafety (www.wiredsafety.org). WiredSafety is a nonprofit group that provides help, information, and education for Internet and mobile device users.

INDEX

PICTURE CREDITS

Cover photo: Image copyright Zsolt Nyulaszi, 2009. Used under license from Shutterstock.com.

Daniel Acker/Bloomberg News/Landov, 7

AP Images, 15, 20, 35, 41, 48, 72, 73, 75

BananaStock/Jupiter Images, 45

© ClassicStock/Alamy, 25

© iStockPhoto.com/Leslie Banks, 32

© iStockPhoto.com/Joselito Briones, 37

© iStockPhoto.com/Michael DeLeon, 88

© iStockPhoto.com/Christine Glade, 56

© iStockPhoto.com/Ermin Gutenberger, 11

© iStockPhoto.com/Edyta Pawloswka, 97

© iStockPhoto.com/George Peters, 28

© iStockPhoto.com/ronen, 69

© iStockPhoto.com/Dra Schwartz, 67

© iStockPhoto.com/Monika Wisniewska, 59

Lucas Jackson/Reuters/Landov, 17

Rob Kim/Landov, 91

Image copyright Monkey Business Images, 2009. Used under license from Shutterstock.com, 52

Newshouse News Service/Landov, 13

Bill O'Connell/Jupiter Images, 100

© Santi Otero/epa/Corbis, 79

© Reuters/Corbis, 82

Image copyright Ronald Sumners, 2009. Used under license from Shutterstock.com, 63

ABOUT THE AUTHOR

Carla Mooney lives in Pittsburgh, Pennsylvania, with her husband and three children. She received her bachelor of economics degree from the University of Pennsylvania. Mooney has written several books and articles for young readers.